ISBN: 9798864394434

Website: www.jdalearning.com

Email: jdalearning@gmail.com

Youtube Educational Videos: www.youtube.com/c/JadyAlvarez

Instagram: www.instagram.com/jadyahomeschool

Numbers 1 - 20
Trace and color the numbers.

Numbers 1- 100
Recite the numbers.

1	2	3	4	5	6	7	8	9	10
11	12	13	14	15	16	17	18	19	20
21	22	23	24	25	26	27	28	29	30
31	32	33	34	35	36	37	38	39	40
41	42	43	44	45	46	47	48	49	50
51	52	53	54	55	56	57	58	59	60
61	62	63	64	65	66	67	68	69	70
71	72	73	74	75	76	77	78	79	80
81	82	83	84	85	86	87	88	89	90
91	92	93	94	95	96	97	98	99	100

Skip Count by 2
Trace and Color the numbers.

Skip Count by 10
Color the numbers on the ladder.

Two-Dimensional Shapes

Pick a color for each shape. Color each shape.

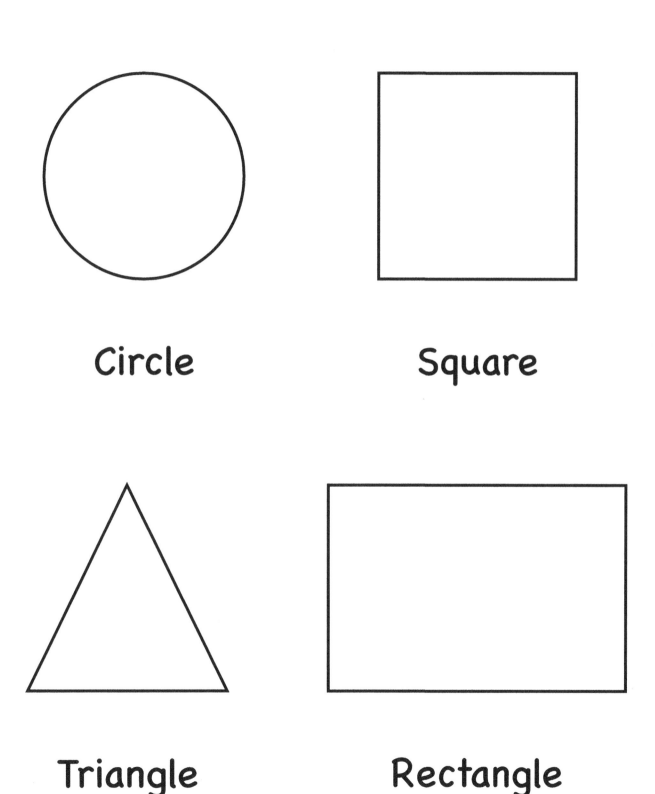

Circle

Square

Triangle

Rectangle

Two-Dimensional Shapes
Pick a color for each shape. Color each shape.

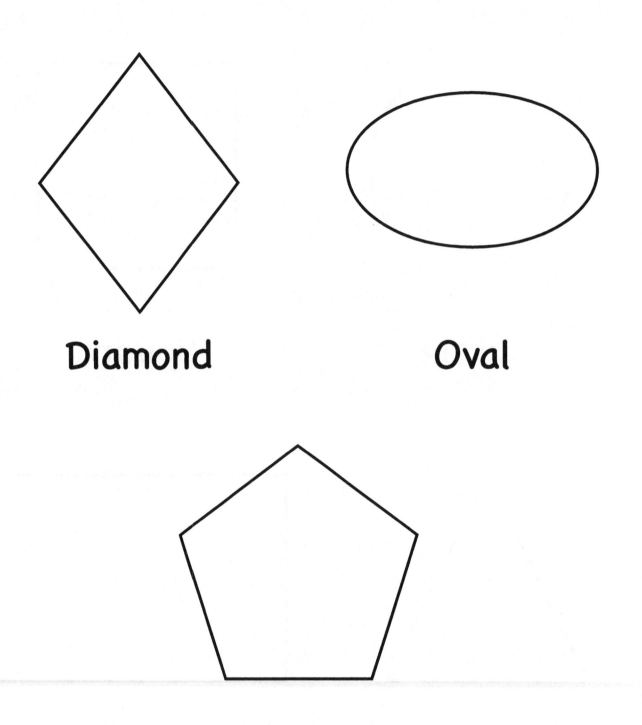

Diamond

Oval

Pentagon

Three-Dimensional Figures

Pick a color for each figure. Color each figure.

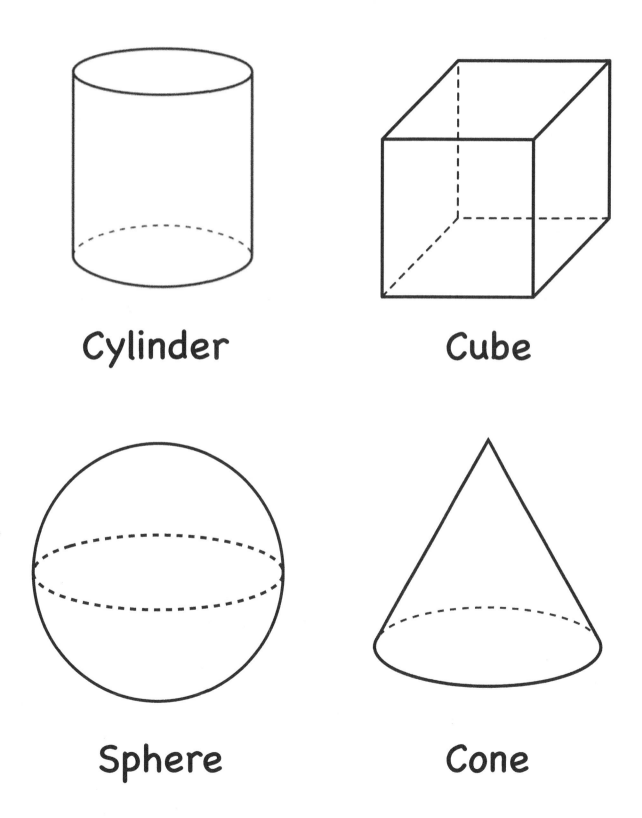

Cylinder

Cube

Sphere

Cone

Time - Clock

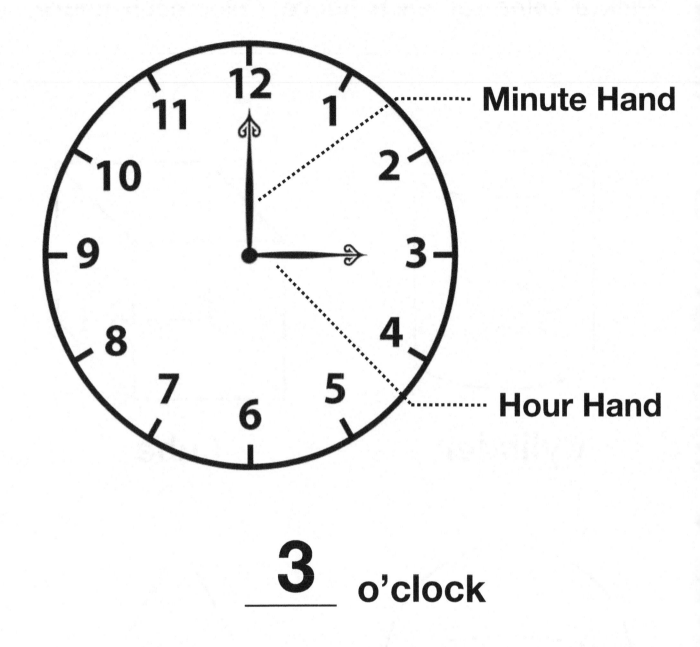

Minute Hand

Hour Hand

__3__ o'clock

The long hand points to the minutes.

The short hand points to the hour.

Time – Digital Clock

Hour   Minute

3 : 00

___ ___

Count and Write

1	2	3	4	5	6	7	8	9	10

   = _____

     = _____

    = _____

     = _____

Count by One
Write the missing numbers.

___ , 2 , 3 , 4 , 5 , 6 , 7 , 8 , 9 , 10

___ , ___ , 3 , 4 , 5 , 6 , 7 , 8 , 9 , 10

1 , ___ , ___ , ___ , 5 , 6 , 7 , 8 , 9 , 10

1 , 2 , ___ , ___ , ___ , 6 , 7 , 8 , 9 , 10

1 , 2 , 3 , ___ , ___ , ___ , 7 , 8 , 9 , 10

Addition
Draw a line to the answer.

🐦 + 🐦 =   4

🌈🌈 + 🌈🌈 =   2

🌼🌼🌼 + 🌼 =   5

☂☂☂ + ☂☂ =   4

Which is more? Circle and color it.

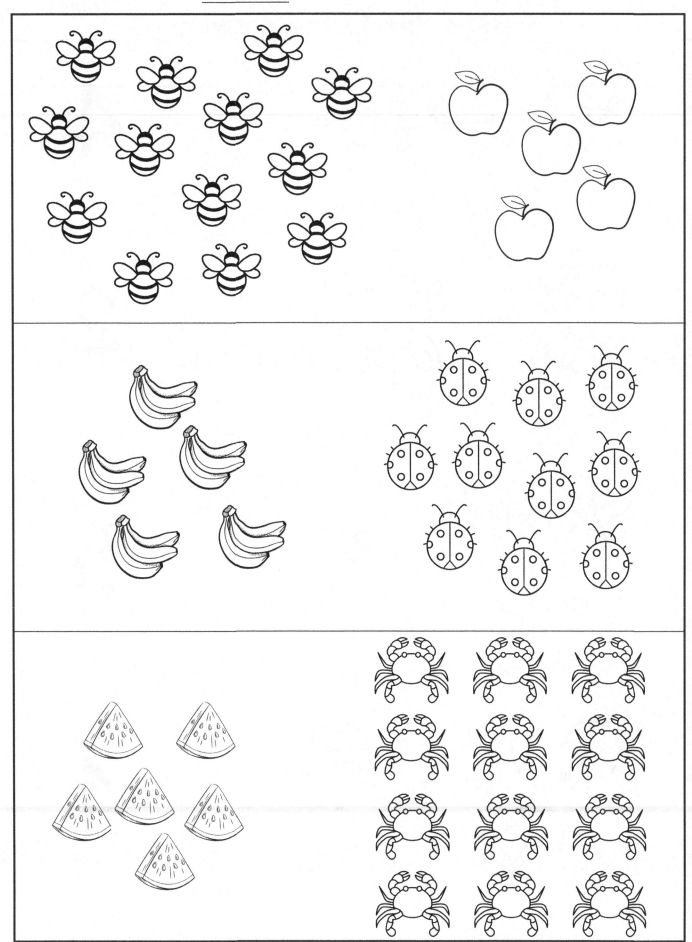

Circle by 2

Position
Which one is in the front? Color it.

Shapes
Cross out (x) the circles.

Count and Write

     = _____

      = _____

 = _____

 = _____

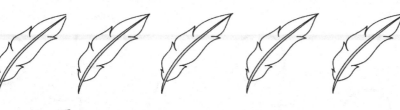 = _____

Count by One
Write the missing numbers.

1 , 2 , 3 , 4 , ___ , ___ , ___ , 8 , 9 , 10

1 , 2 , 3 , 4 , 5 , ___ , ___ , ___ , 9 , 10

1 , 2 , 3 , 4 , 5 , 6 , ___ , ___ , ___ , 10

1 , 2 , 3 , 4 , 5 , 6 , 7 , ___ , ___ , ___

Addition
Draw a line to the answer.

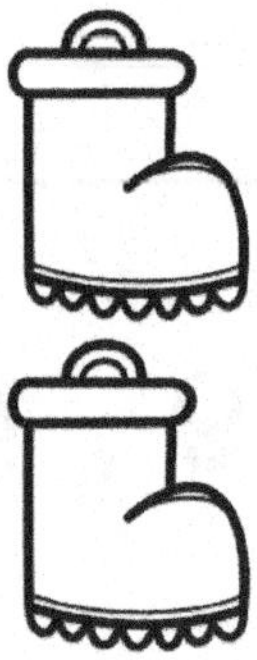

+ =   **5**

+ =   **6**

+ =   **3**

+ =   **6**

Which is less? Circle and color it.

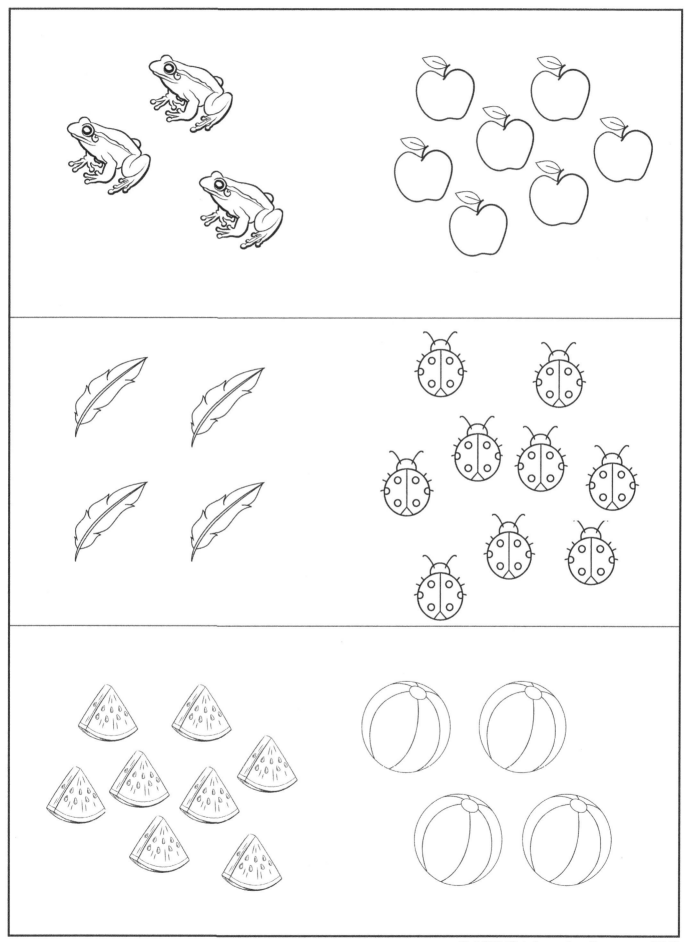

Circle by 3

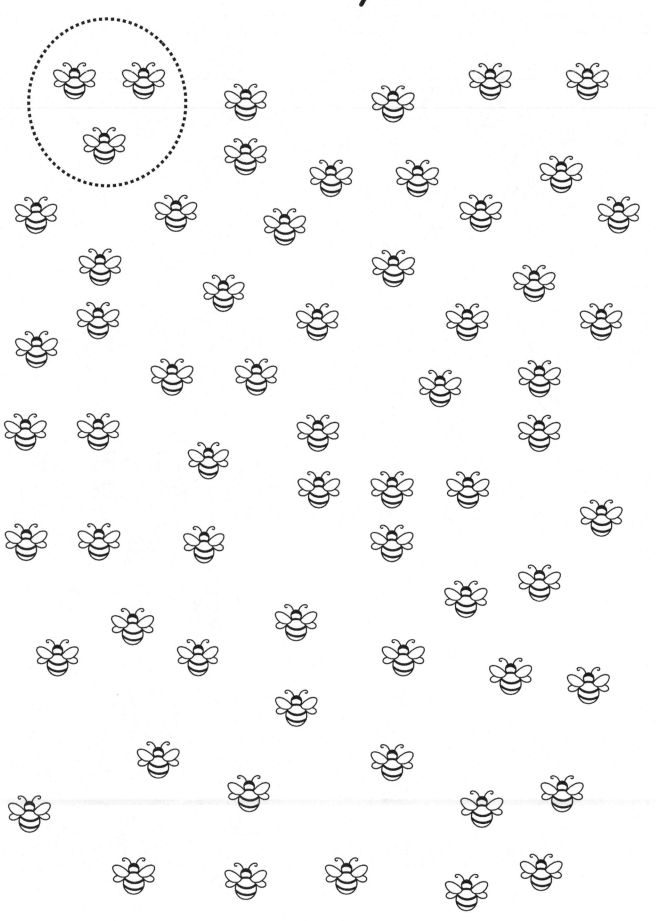

Position
Which one is in the back? Color it.

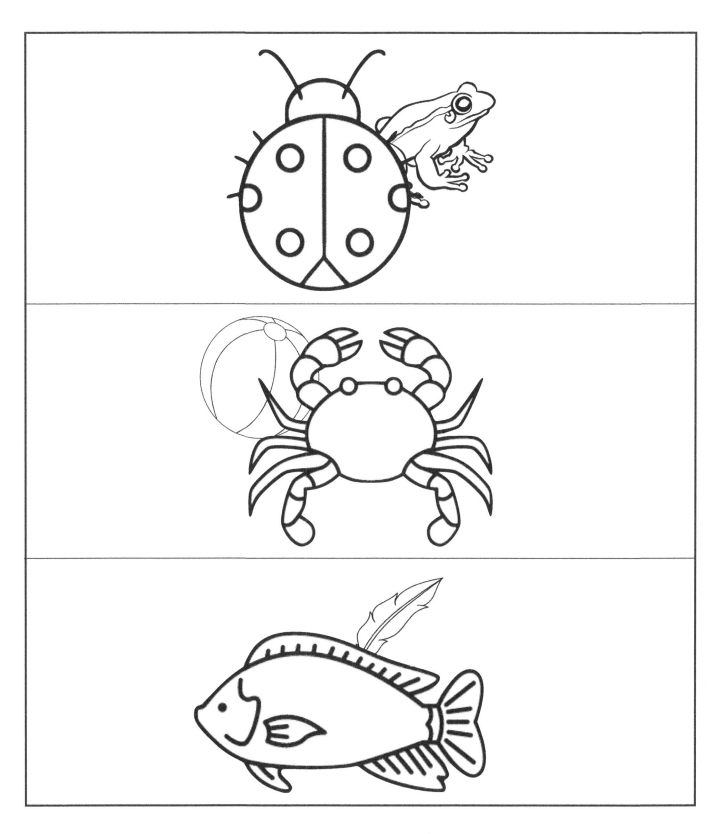

Shapes
Color the triangles.

Count and Write

| 1 | 2 | 3 | 4 | 5 | 6 | 7 | 8 | 9 | 10 |

= _____

= _____

= _____

= _____

= _____

Count by One
Write the missing numbers.

___ , 2 , ___ , ___ , 5 , 6 , ___ , 8 , ___ , 10

1 , ___ , 3 , 4 , ___ , ___ , 7 , ___ , 9 , ___

___ , ___ , 3 , ___ , 5 , 6 , ___ , ___ , 9 , 10

Addition
Draw a line to the answer.

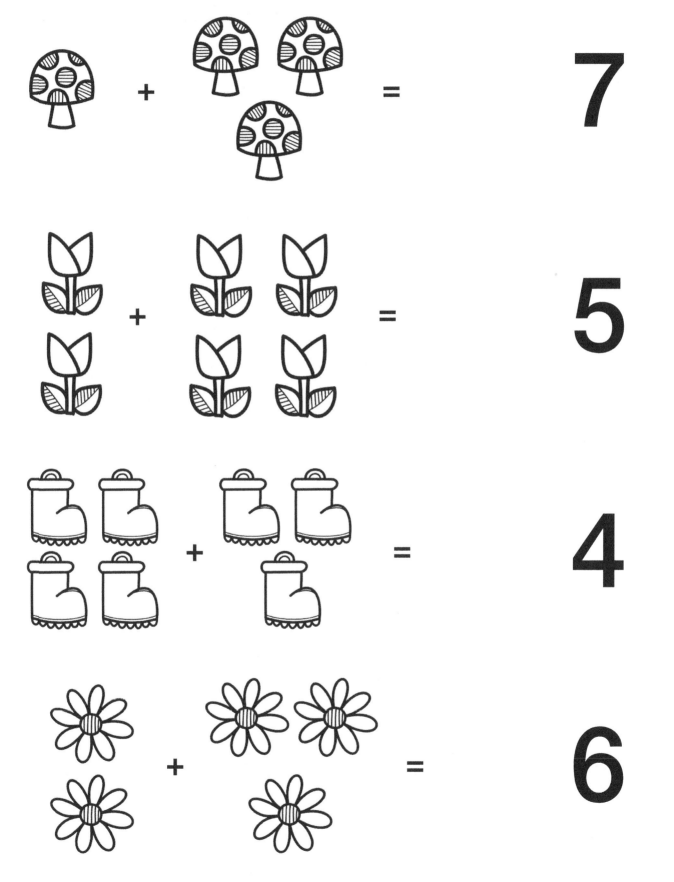

Which is <u>more</u>? Circle and color it.

Circle by 4

Position
Which one is on top? Color it.

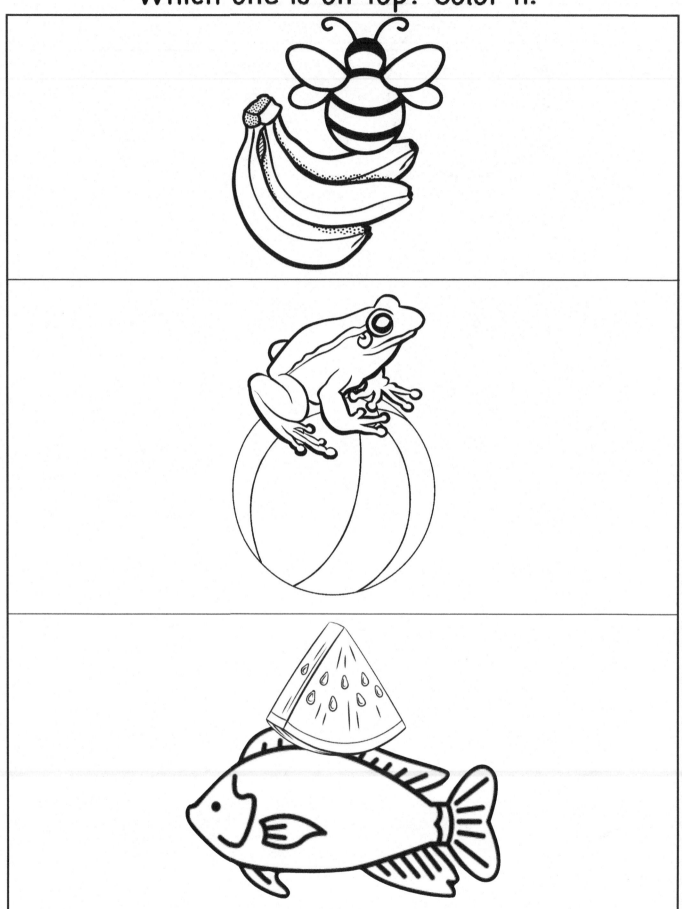

Shapes
Cross out (x) the squares.

Count and Write

| 1 | 2 | 3 | 4 | 5 | 6 | 7 | 8 | 9 | 10 |

 = _____

 = _____

 = _____

 = _____

 = _____

Count by One
Write the missing numbers.

1 , 2 , ___ , ___ , 5 , ___ , 7 , ___ , 9 , ___

1 , ___ , 3 , ___ , 5 , ___ , 7 , ___ , 9 , ___

___ , ___ , 3 , ___ , 5 , 6 , ___ , ___ , 9 , 10

Addition
Draw a line to the answer.

$=$ **8**

+

_____   _____

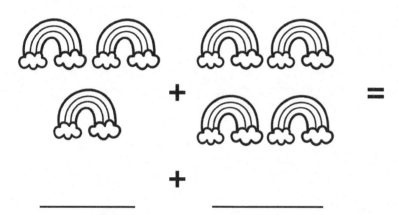

$=$ **6**

+

_____   _____

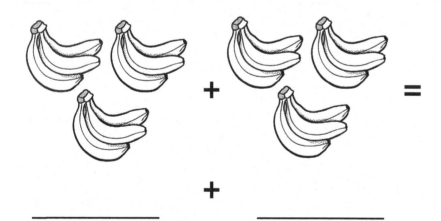

$=$ **5**

+

_____   _____

 +  $=$ **7**

+

_____   _____

Which is less? Circle and color it.

Circle by 5

Position
Which one is on the bottom? Color it.

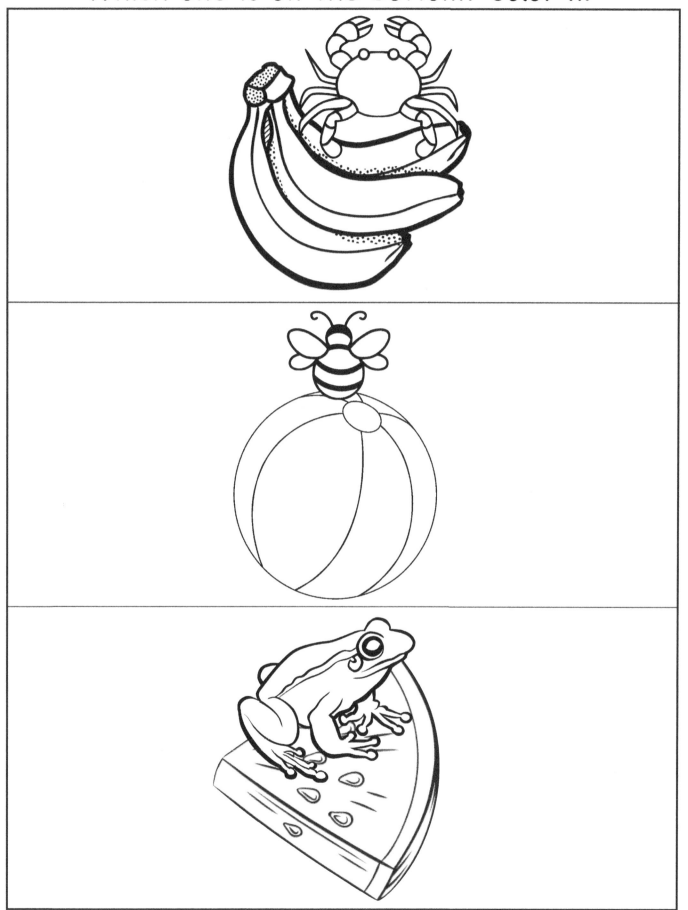

Shapes
Color the circles.

Count and Write

| 1 | 2 | 3 | 4 | 5 | 6 | 7 | 8 | 9 | 10 |

= _____

= _____

= _____

= _____

= _____

Count by Two
Write the missing numbers.

___ , 4 , 6 , 8 , 10 , 12 , 14 , 16 , 18 , 20

___ , ___ , 6 , 8 , 10 , 12 , 14 , 16 , 18 , 20

2 , ___ , ___ , ___ , 10 , 12 , 14 , 16 , 18 , 20

2 , 4 , ___ , ___ , ___ , 12 , 14 , 16 , 18 , 20

2 , 4 , 6 , ___ , ___ , ___ , 14 , 16 , 18 , 20

Which is different? Circle it.

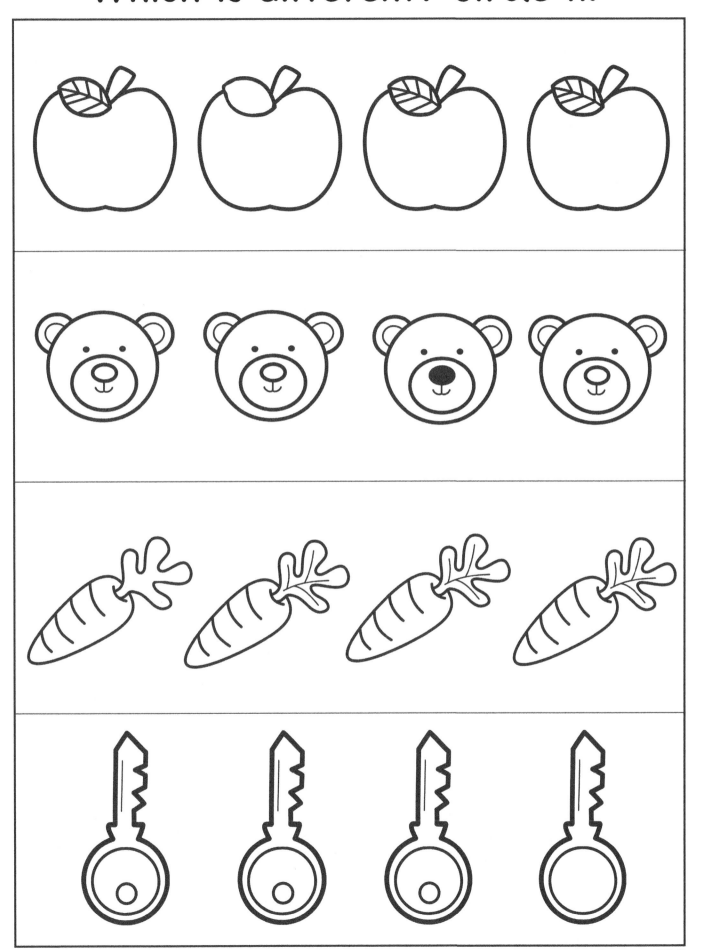

Addition
Draw a line to the answer.

$+$

_____ $=$ **10**

_____   _____

$+$

_____ $=$ **9**

_____   _____

$+$

_____ $=$ **7**

_____   _____

$+$ $=$ **8**

$+$

_____   _____

Ordinal Numbers

Circle the <u>first</u> object in the row.

Circle the <u>second</u> object in the row.

Circle the <u>third</u> object in the row.

Position

Cross out the picture on the <u>left</u>.

Color the picture in the <u>middle</u>.

Circle the picture on the <u>right</u>.

Shapes
Cross out (x) the triangles.

Count and Write

1	2	3	4	5	6	7	8	9	10

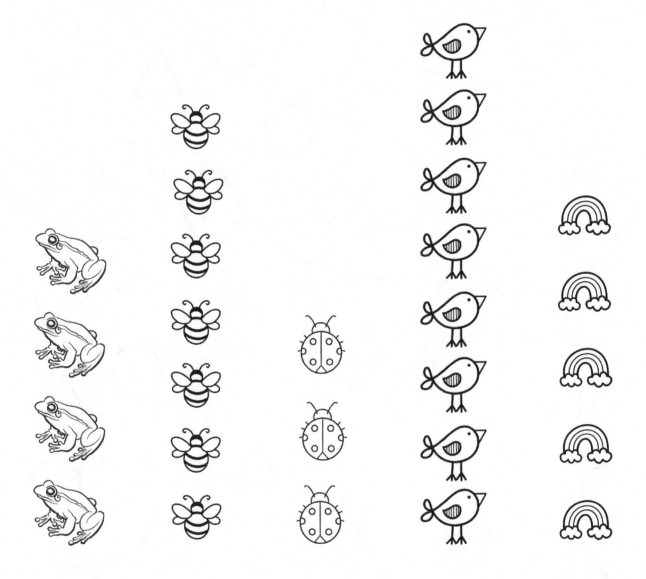

___ ___ ___ ___ ___ ___

Count by Two
Write the missing numbers.

2 , 4 , 6 , 8 , ___ , ___ , ___ , 16 , 18 , 20

2 , 4 , 6 , 8 , 10 , ___ , ___ , ___ , 18 , 20

2 , 4 , 6 , 8 , 10 , 12 , ___ , ___ , ___ , 20

2 , 4 , 6 , 8 , 10 , 12 , 14 , ___ , ___ , ___

Which is different? Circle it.

Addition
Draw a line to the answer.

🐦🐦🐦 🐦 + 🐦 = **7**
🐦🐦🐦

_____ + _____

🌈🌈🌈🌈 + 🌈 = **10**
🌈🌈🌈🌈

_____ + _____

🍌🍌🍌 + 🍌🍌 = **8**
🍌🍌 🍌

_____ + _____

☂☂ + ☂☂☂ = **9**
☂☂ ☂☂☂

_____ + _____

Ordinal Numbers

Circle the <u>second</u> object in the row.

Circle the <u>first</u> object in the row.

Circle the <u>third</u> object in the row.

Position

Cross out the picture on the <u>left</u>.

Color the picture in the <u>middle</u>.

Circle the picture on the <u>right</u>.

Shapes
Color the squares.

Count and Write

_____

_____

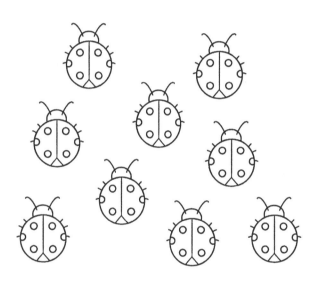

_____

_____

_____

_____

Count by Two
Write the missing numbers.

___ , 4 , ___ , ___ , 10 , 12 , ___ , 16 , ___ , 20

___ , ___ , 6 , ___ , 10 , 12 , ___ , ___ , 18 , 20

2 , ___ , 6 , 8 , ___ , ___ , 14 , ___ , 18 , ___

Which is different? Circle it.

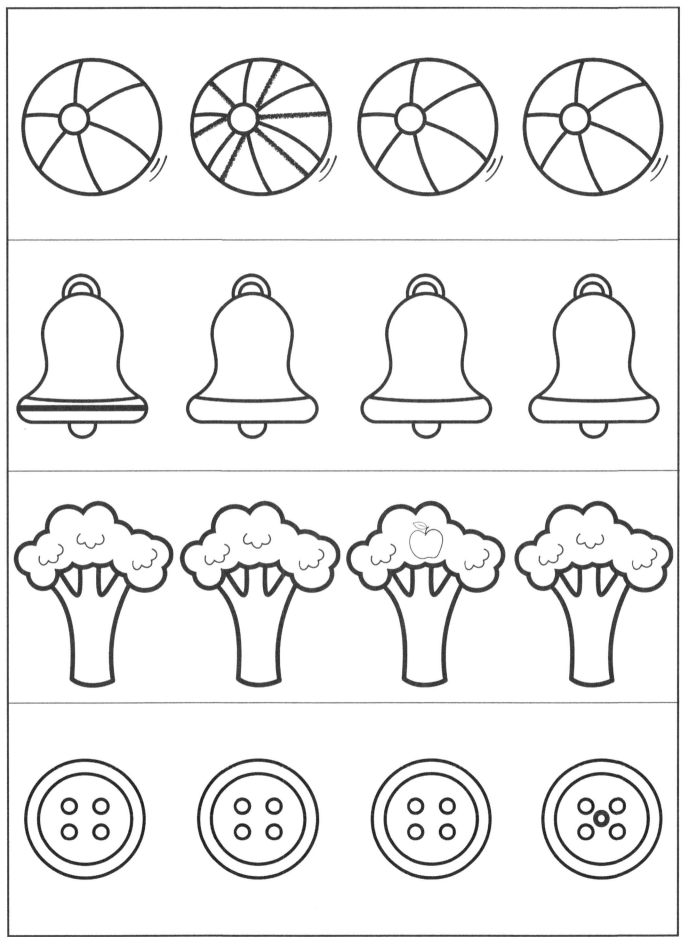

Addition

__1__ + __1__ = ___

___ + ___ = ___

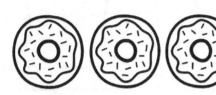

___ + ___ = ___

___ + ___ = ___

___ + ___ = ___

___ + ___ = ___

Ordinal Numbers

Circle the <u>third</u> object in the row.

Circle the <u>first</u> object in the row.

Circle the <u>second</u> object in the row.

Circle the <u>fourth</u> object in the row.

Position

Cross out the picture on the <u>left</u>.

Color the picture in the <u>middle</u>.

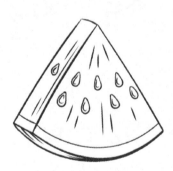  

Circle the picture on the <u>right</u>.

Shapes
Cross out (x) the pentagons.

Count and Write

Count by Two
Write the missing numbers.

2 , 4 , ___ , ___ , 10 , ___ , 14 , ___ , 18 , ___

___ , ___ , 6 , ___ , 10 , 12 , ___ , ___ , 18 , 20

2 , ___ , 6 , ___ , 10 , ___ , 14 , ___ , 18 , ___

Which is different? Circle it.

Addition

__ + __ = __

__ + __ = __

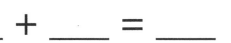

__ + __ = __

__ + __ = __

__ + __ = __

__ + __ = __

Ordinal Numbers

Circle the <u>fourth</u> object in the row.

Circle the <u>second</u> object in the row.

Circle the <u>third</u> object in the row.

Circle the <u>first</u> object in the row.

Position

Cross out the picture on the <u>left</u>.

Color the picture in the <u>middle</u>.

Circle the picture on the <u>right</u>.

Shapes
Color the rectangles.

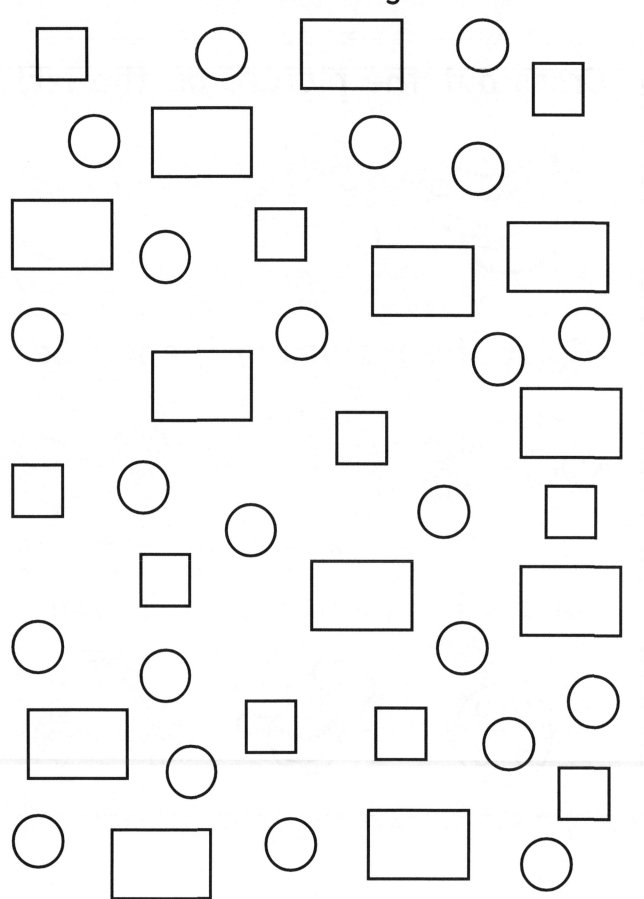

Count by Two and Write

| 1 | 2 | 3 | 4 | 5 | 6 | 7 | 8 | 9 | 10 |

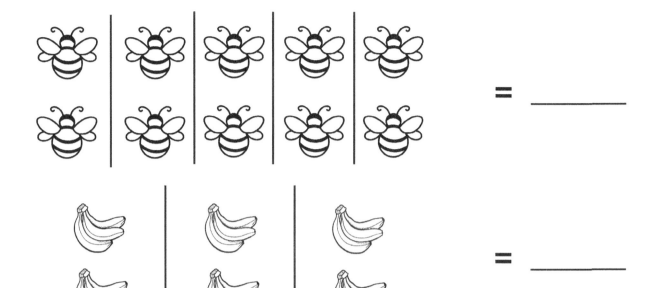

= _____

= _____

= _____

= _____

= _____

Count by Ten
Write the missing numbers.

___ , 20 , 30 , 40 , 50 , 60 , 70 , 80 , 90 , 100

___ , ___ , 30 , 40 , 50 , 60 , 70 , 80 , 90 , 100

10 , ___ , ___ , ___ , 50 , 60 , 70 , 80 , 90 , 100

10 , 20 , ___ , ___ , ___ , 60 , 70 , 80 , 90 , 100

10 , 20 , 30 , ___ , ___ , ___ , 70 , 80 , 90 , 100

How many sides?

Draw a line to the answer.

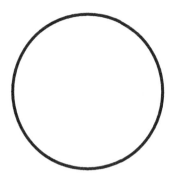

4

0

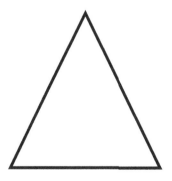

4

3

© 2023 JDA Learning Resources LLC

Addition

___ + ___ = ___

___ + ___ = ___

___ + ___ = ___

___ + ___ = ___

___ + ___ = ___

___ + ___ = ___

Position

Cross out the picture on the <u>left</u>.

Color the picture in the <u>middle</u>.

 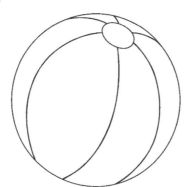 

Circle the picture on the <u>right</u>.

Telling Time by the Hour

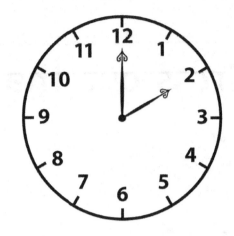

_____ o'clock   _____ o'clock

_____ o'clock   _____ o'clock

Shapes
Cross out (x) the diamonds.

Draw a House

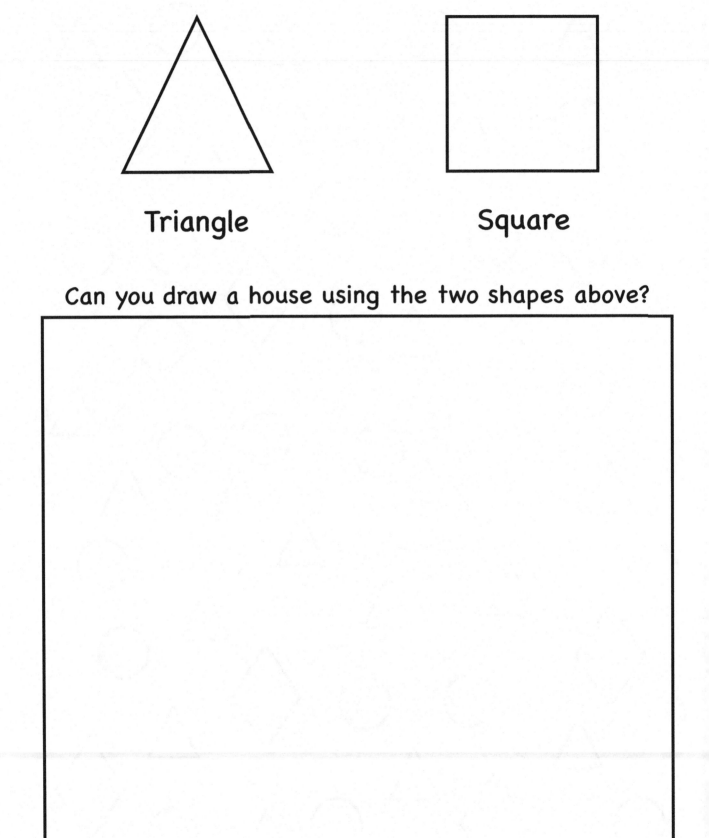

Triangle

Square

Can you draw a house using the two shapes above?

Shapes Data Collection
Color the rectangles.

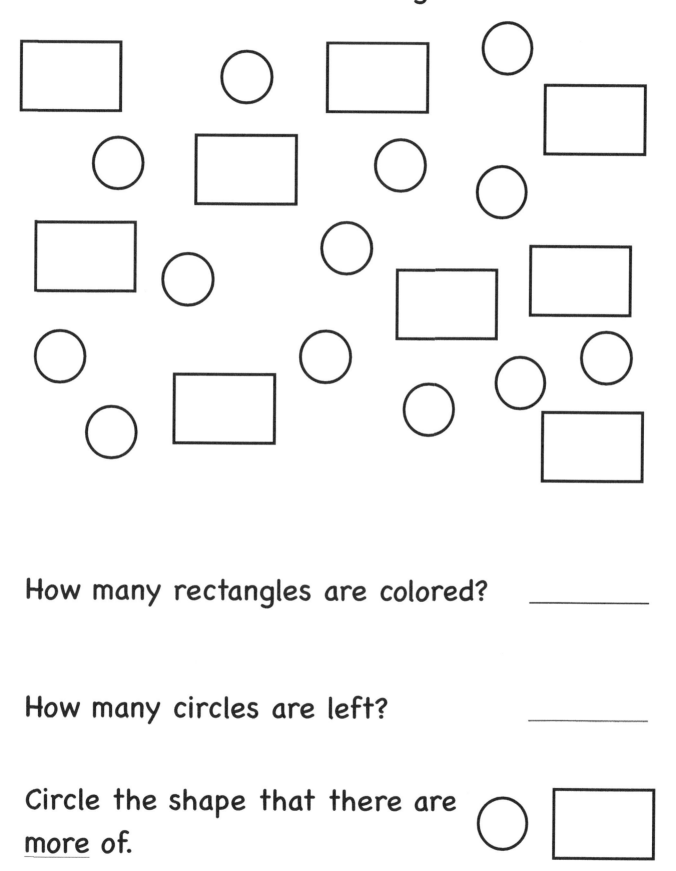

How many rectangles are colored? _____

How many circles are left? _____

Circle the shape that there are
more of.

Addition

__ + __ = __

__ + __ = __

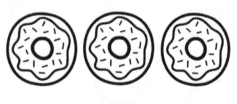

__ + __ = __

__ + __ = __

__ + __ = __

__ + __ = __

Count by Ten
Write the missing numbers.

10 , 20 , 30 , 40 , ___ , ___ , ___ , 80 , 90 , 100

10 , 20 , 30 , 40 , 50 , ___ , ___ , ___ , 90 , 100

10 , 20 , 30 , 40 , 50 , 60 , ___ , ___ , ___ , 100

10 , 20 , 30 , 40 , 50 , 60 , 70 , ___ , ___ , ___

Shapes
How many sides? Draw a line to the answer.

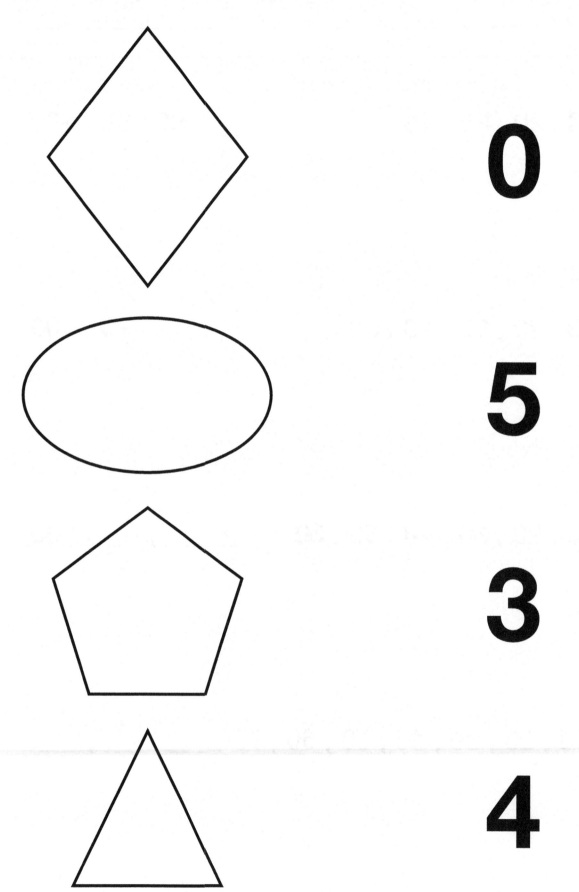

0

5

3

4

Measurement

Which is longer? Color it.

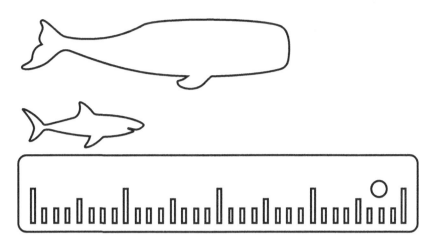

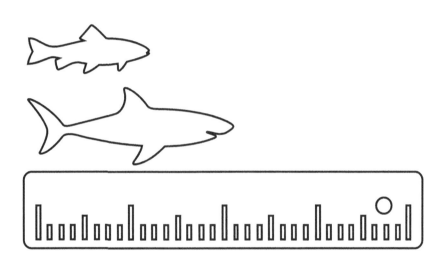

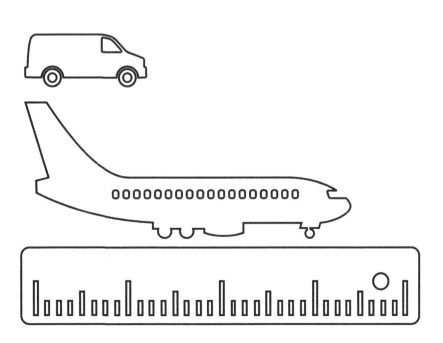

Shapes
Color the pentagons.

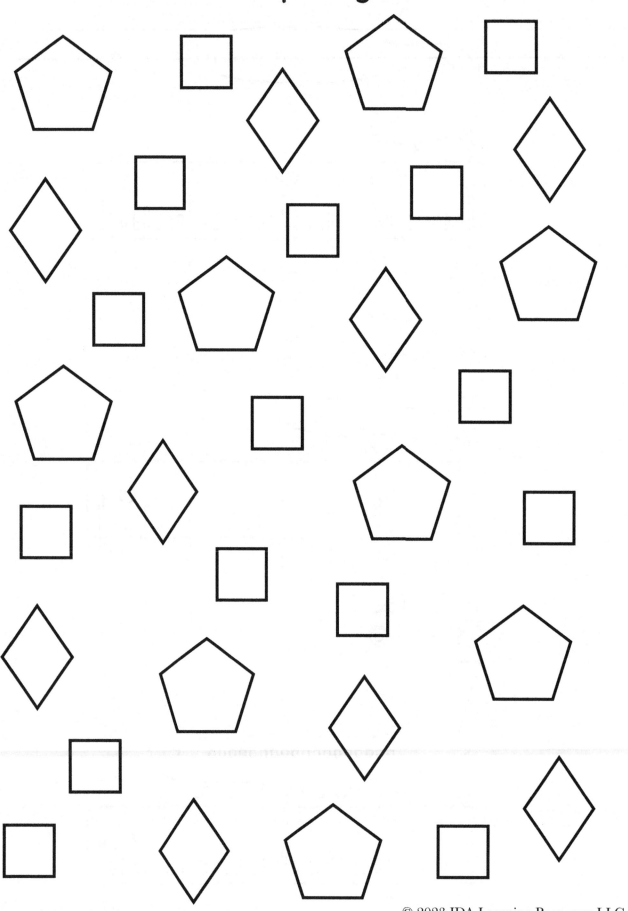

Telling Time by the Hour

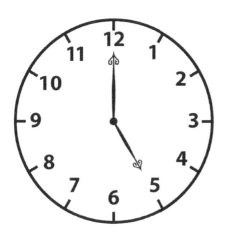

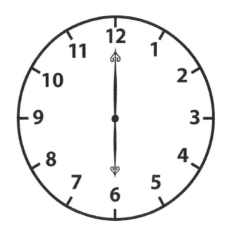

_____ o'clock

_____ o'clock

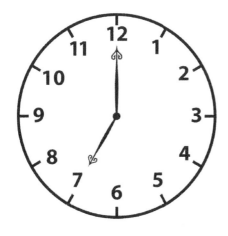

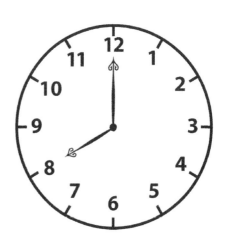

_____ o'clock

_____ o'clock

Draw a Car

Circle

Rectangle

Can you draw a car using the two shapes above?

Shapes Data Collection

Cross out (x) the circles.

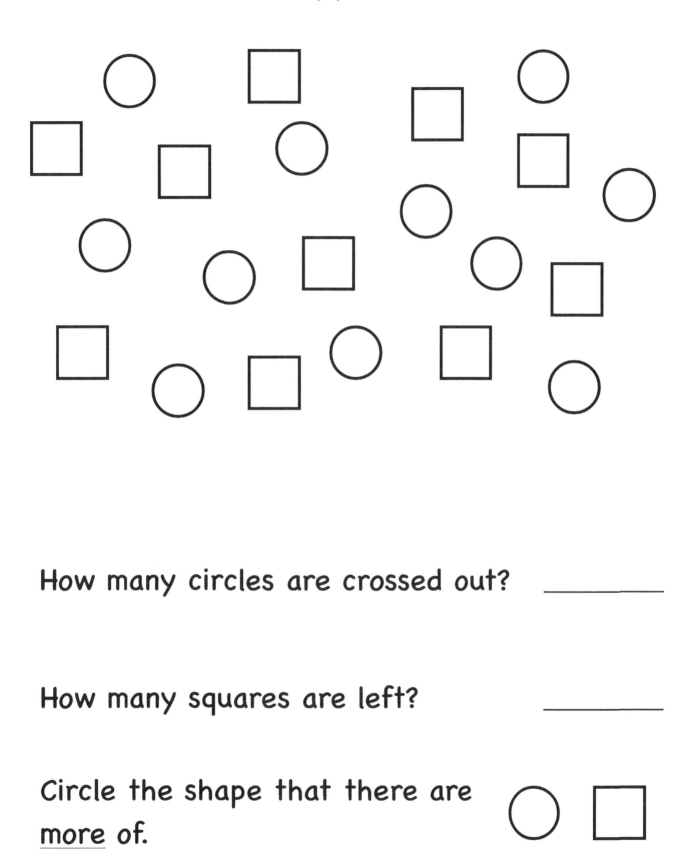

How many circles are crossed out? _____

How many squares are left? _____

Circle the shape that there are
more of. ○ □

Cross out 1. How many are left?

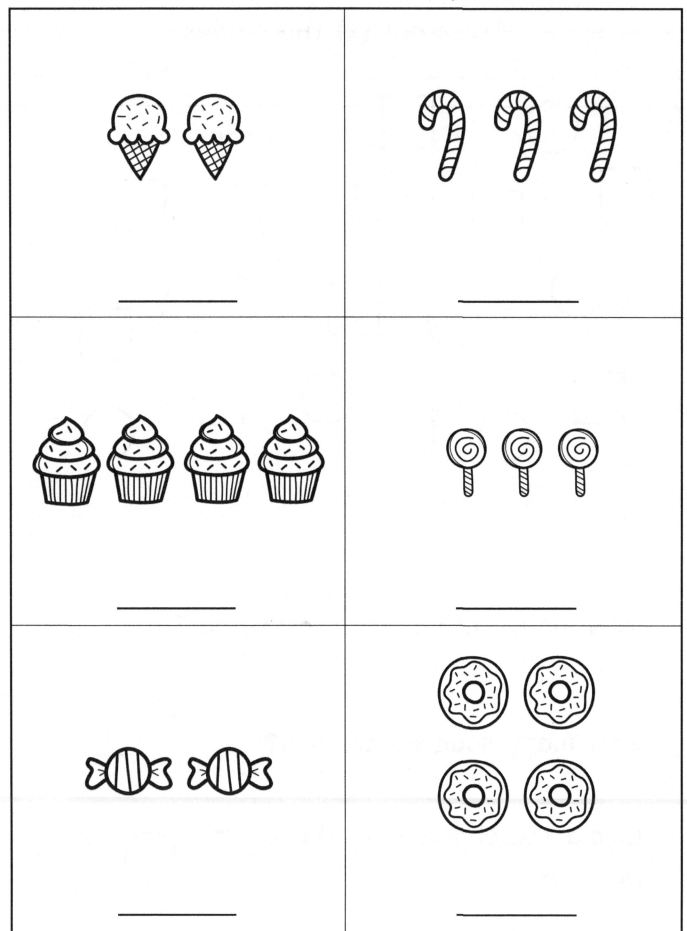

Count by Ten

Write the missing numbers.

___ , 20 , ___ , ___ , 50 , 60 , ___ , 80 , ___ , 100

10 , ___ , 30 , 40 , ___ , ___ , 70 , ___ , 90 , ___

___ , ___ , 30 , ___ , 50 , 60 , ___ , ___ , 90 , 100

Shapes
How many corners? Draw a line to the answer.

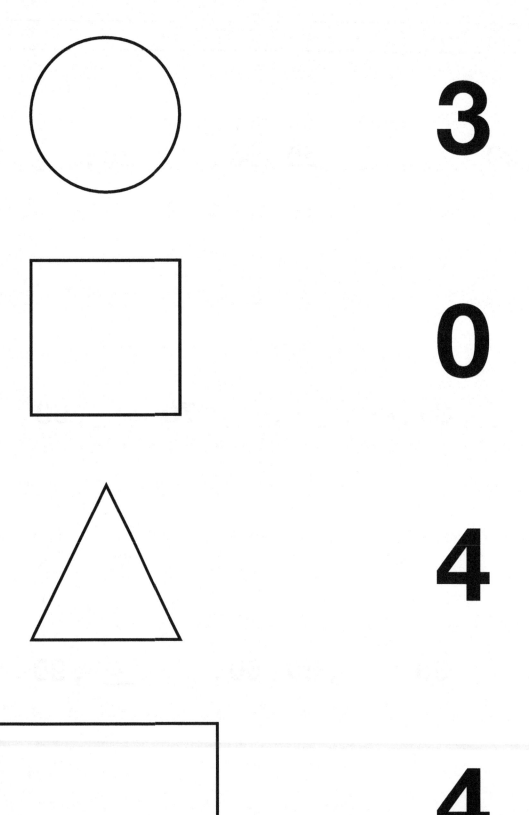

3

0

4

4

Measurement
Which is shorter? Circle it.

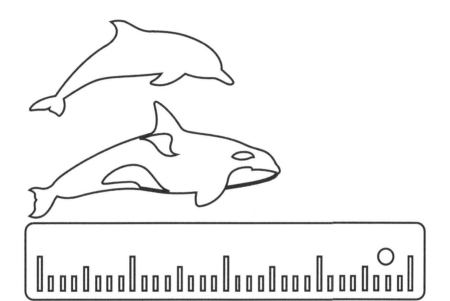

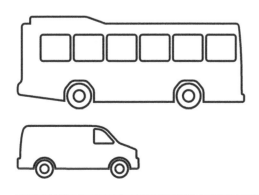

Shapes

Cross out (x) the ovals.

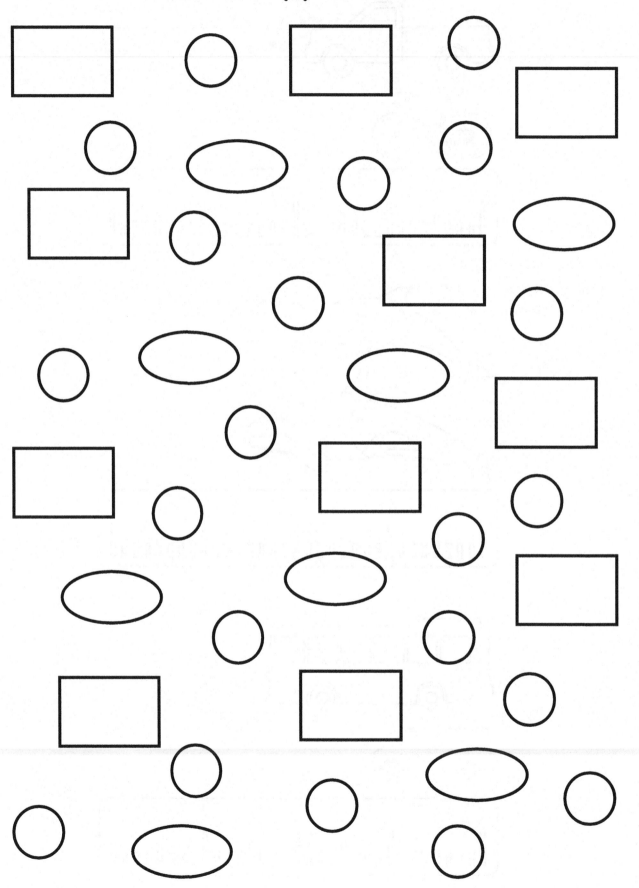

Telling Time by the Hour

_____ o'clock   _____ o'clock

_____ o'clock   _____ o'clock

Draw a Lollipop

Circle

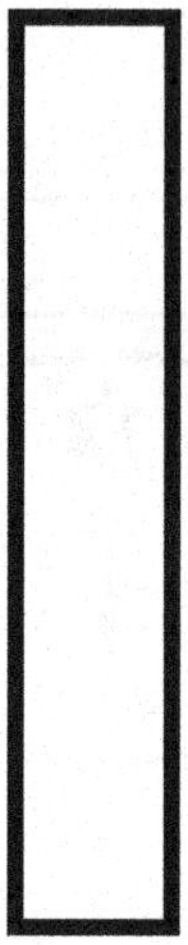

Rectangle

Can you draw a lollipop using the two shapes above?

Shapes Data Collection
Color the squares.

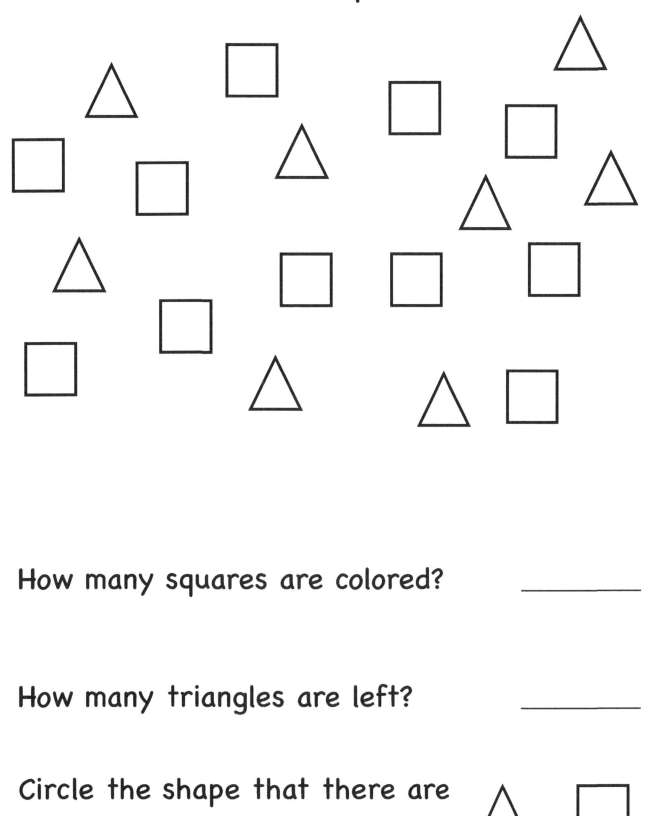

How many squares are colored?   _____

How many triangles are left?   _____

Circle the shape that there are less of.

Cross out 2. How many are left?

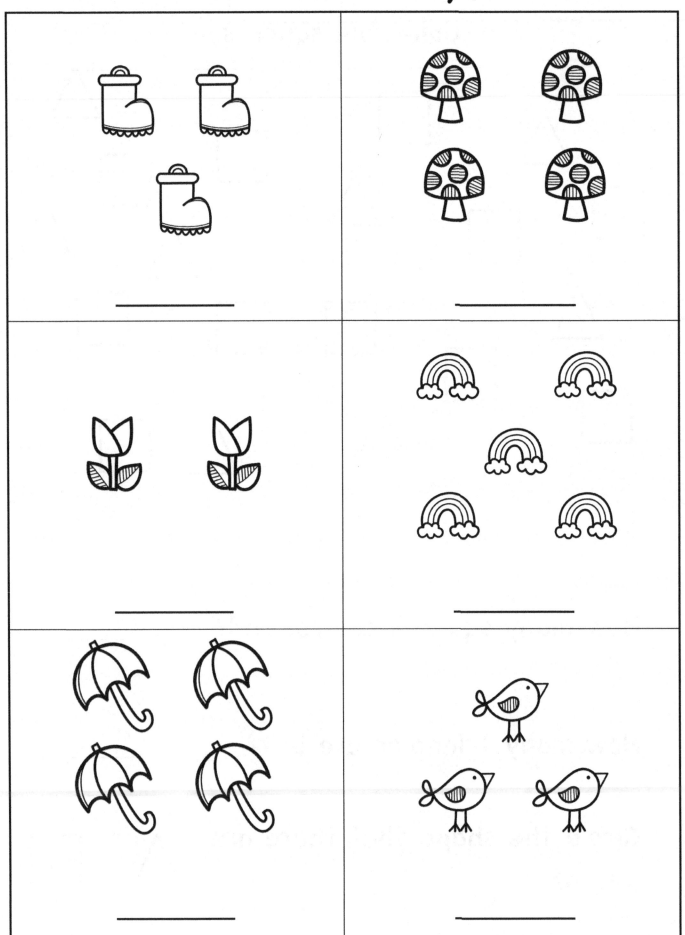

Count by Ten
Write the missing numbers.

10 , 20 , ___ , ___ , 50 , ___ , 70 , ___ , 90 , ___

10 , ___ , 30 , ___ , 50 , ___ , 70 , ___ , 90 , ___

___ , ___ , 30 , ___ , 50 , 60 , ___ , ___ , 90 , 100

Shapes

How many corners? Draw a line to the answer.

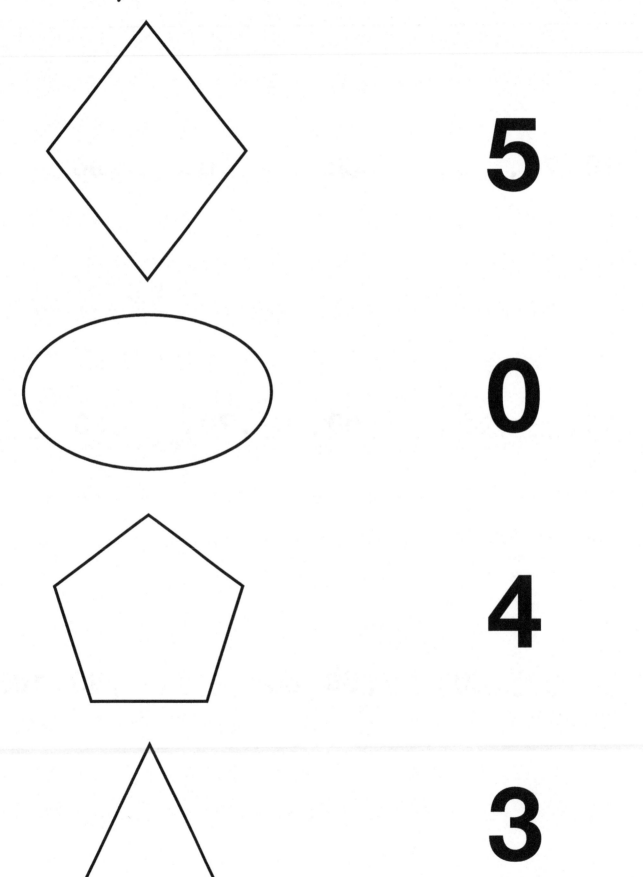

5

0

4

3

Measurement
Which is taller? Color it.

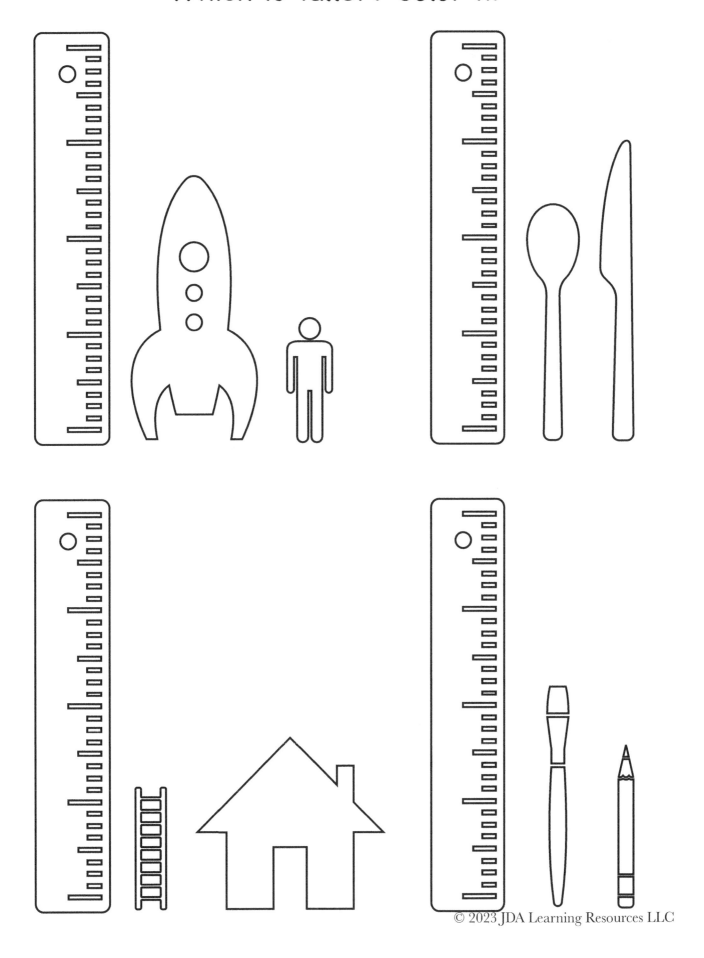

Shapes
Color the diamonds.

Telling Time by the Hour

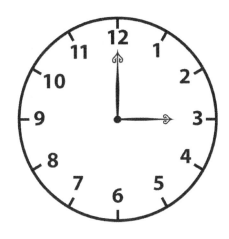

_____ o'clock

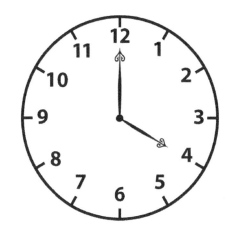

_____ o'clock

_____ o'clock

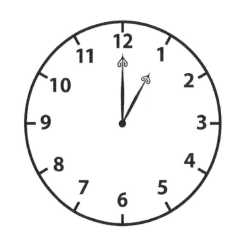

_____ o'clock

Draw a Rocket Ship

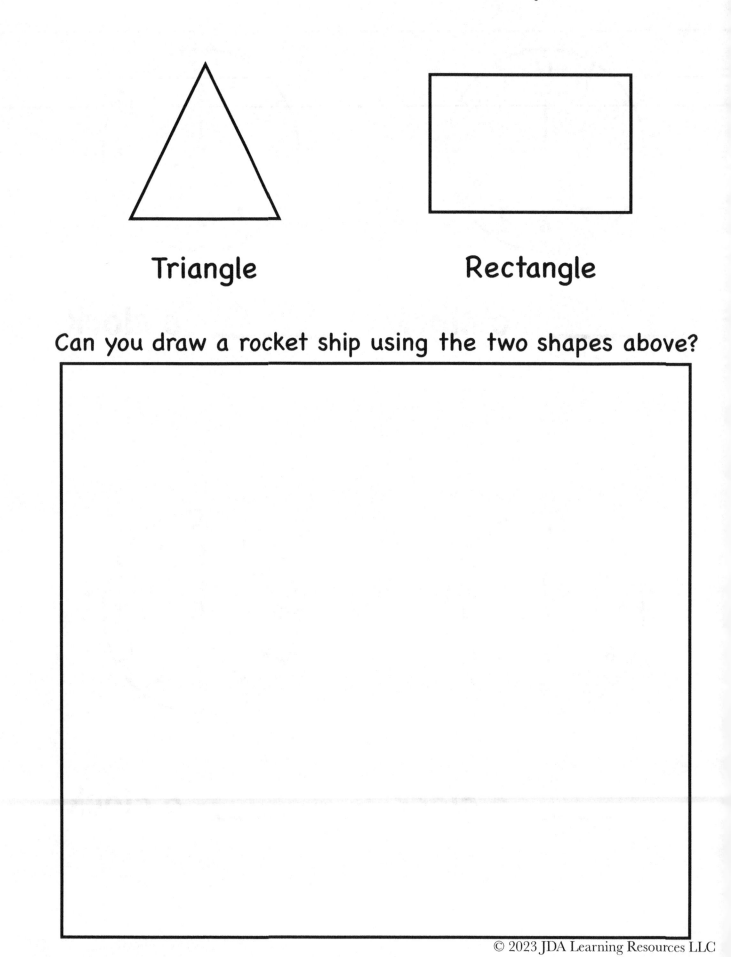

Triangle

Rectangle

Can you draw a rocket ship using the two shapes above?

Shapes Data Collection

Cross out (x) the ovals.

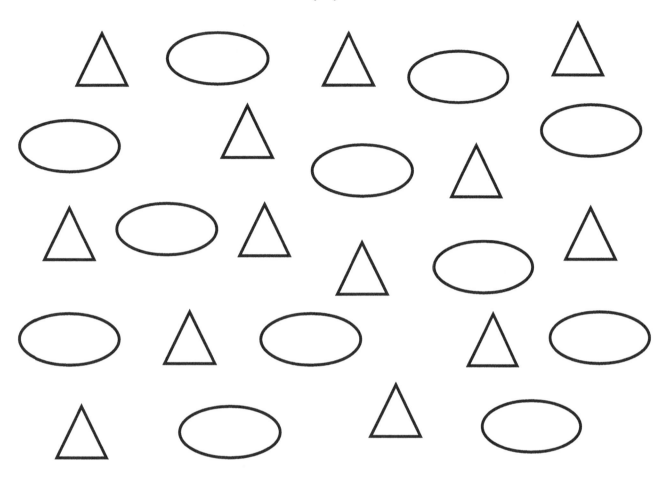

How many ovals are crossed out? _____

How many triangles are left? _____

Circle the shape that there are
more of.

Cross out 3. How many are left?

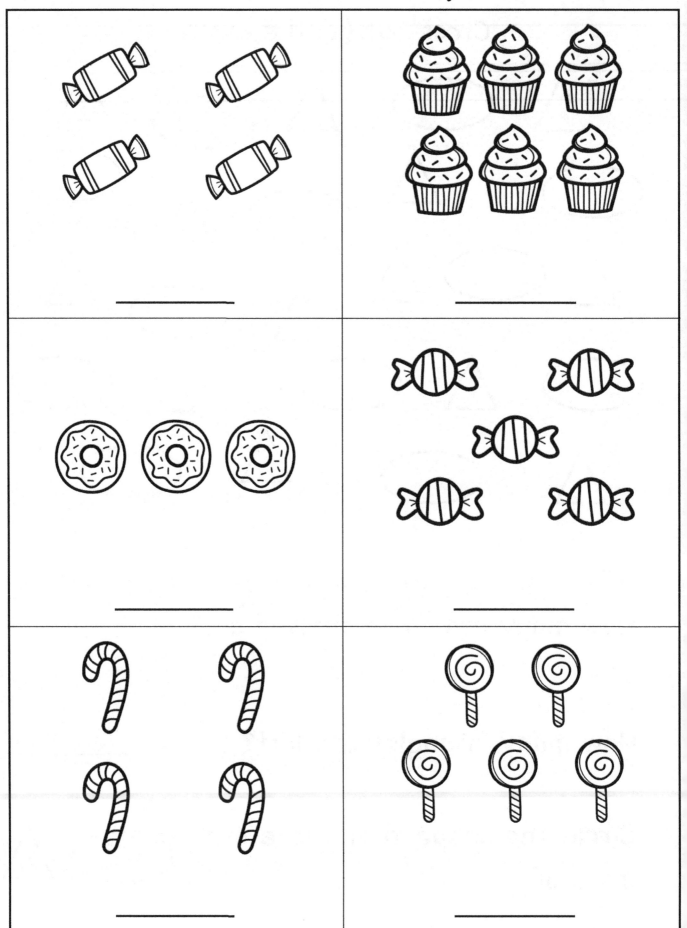

Count Backward by One
Write the missing numbers.

10 , 9 , 8 , 7 , 6 , 5 , 4 , 3 , 2 , ___

10 , 9 , 8 , 7 , 6 , 5 , 4 , 3 , ___ , ___

10 , 9 , 8 , 7 , 6 , 5 , ___ , ___ , ___ , 1

10 , 9 , 8 , 7 , 6 , ___ , ___ , ___ , 2 , 1

10 , 9 , 8 , 7 , ___ , ___ , ___ , 3 , 2 , 1

Measurement
Which is shorter? Circle it.

What comes next? Color it.

Figures
Cross out (x) the cubes.

Telling Time by the Hour

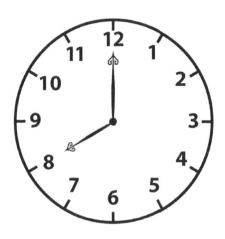

_____ o'clock

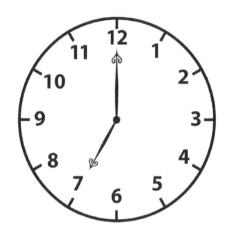

_____ o'clock

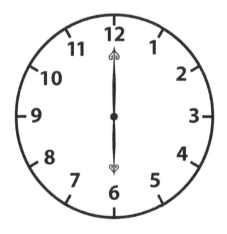

_____ o'clock

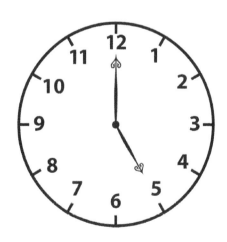

_____ o'clock

Draw a Flag

Rectangle   Rectangle

Can you draw a flag using the two shapes above?

Figures Data Collection
Color the cubes.

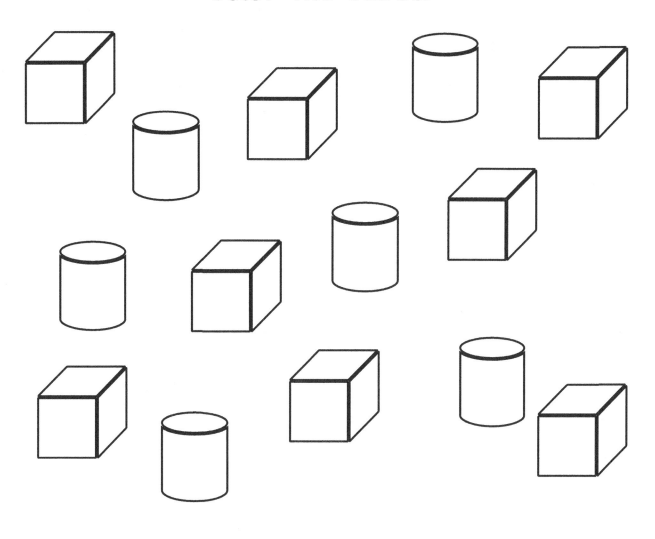

How many cubes are colored?   _____

How many cylinders are left?   _____

Circle the figure that there are less of.

Cross out 4. How many are left?

Count Backward by One
Write the missing numbers.

10 , 9 , 8 , ___ , ___ , ___ , 4 , 3 , 2 , 1

10 , 9 , ___ , ___ , ___ , 5 , 4 , 3 , 2 , 1

10 , ___ , ___ , ___ , 6 , 5 , 4 , 3 , 2 , 1

___ , ___ , ___ , 7 , 6 , 5 , 4 , 3 , 2 , 1

Measurement
Cross out (x) the shortest. Color the tallest.

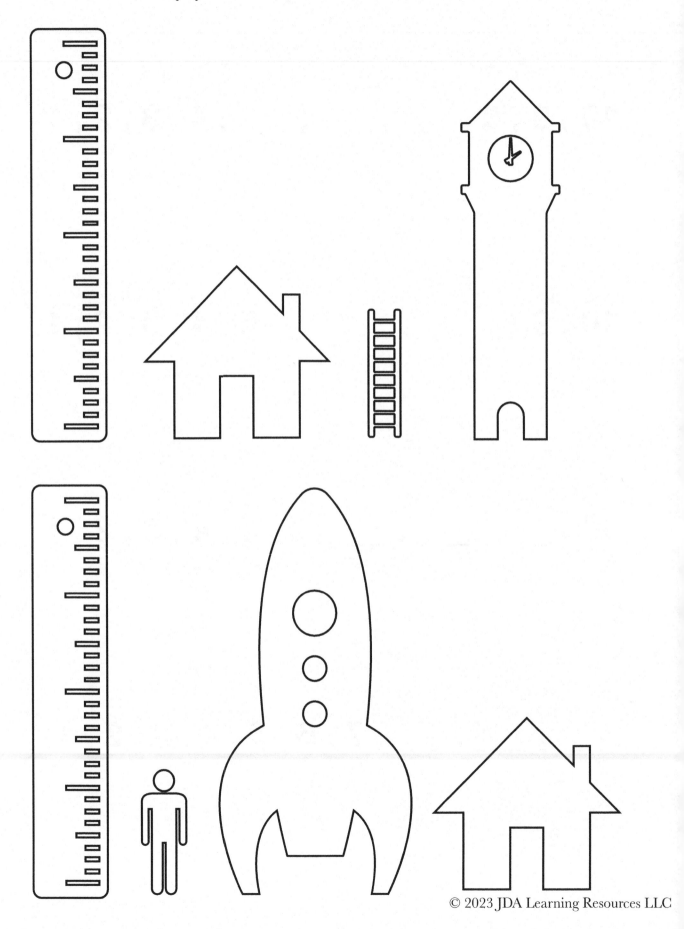

What comes next? Circle it.

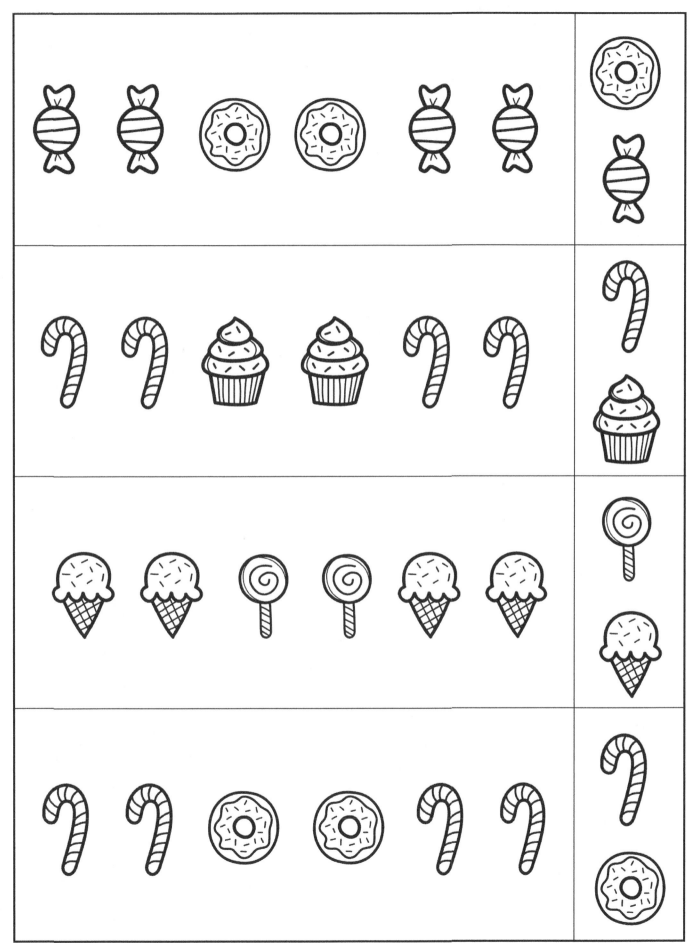

Figures

Color the cones.

Telling Time by the Hour

_____ o'clock

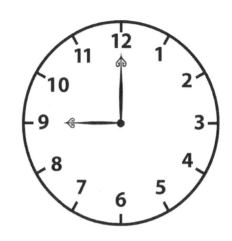

_____ o'clock

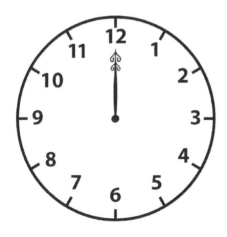

_____ o'clock

_____ o'clock

Draw a Sailboat

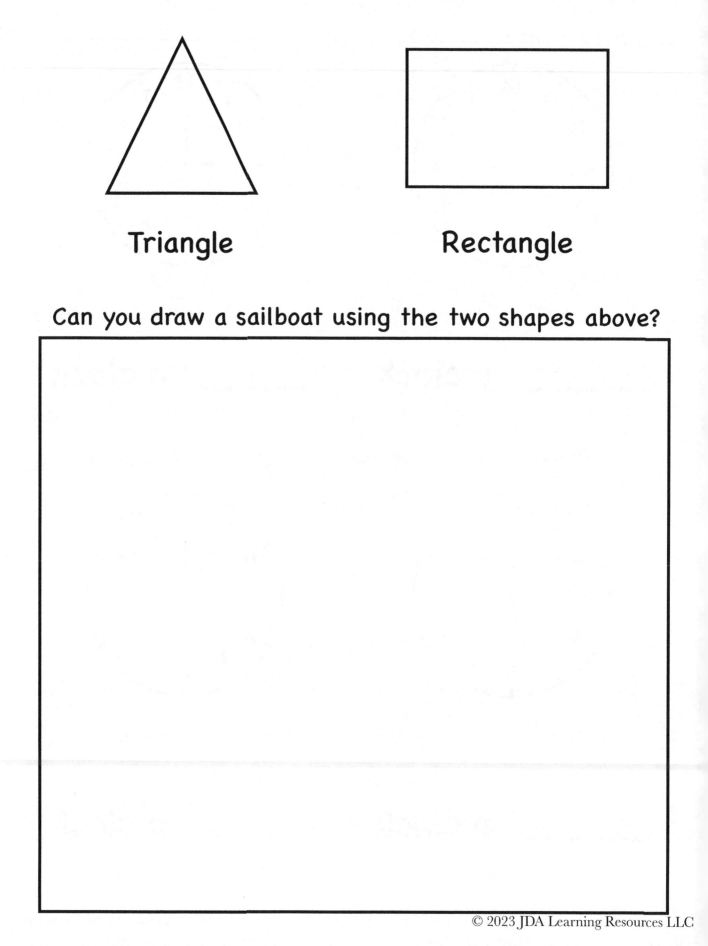

Triangle

Rectangle

Can you draw a sailboat using the two shapes above?

Figures Data Collection

Cross out (x) the spheres.

How many spheres are crossed out? _____

How many cones are left? _____

Circle the figure that there are
<u>less</u> of.

 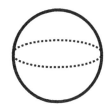

Cross out 5. How many are left?

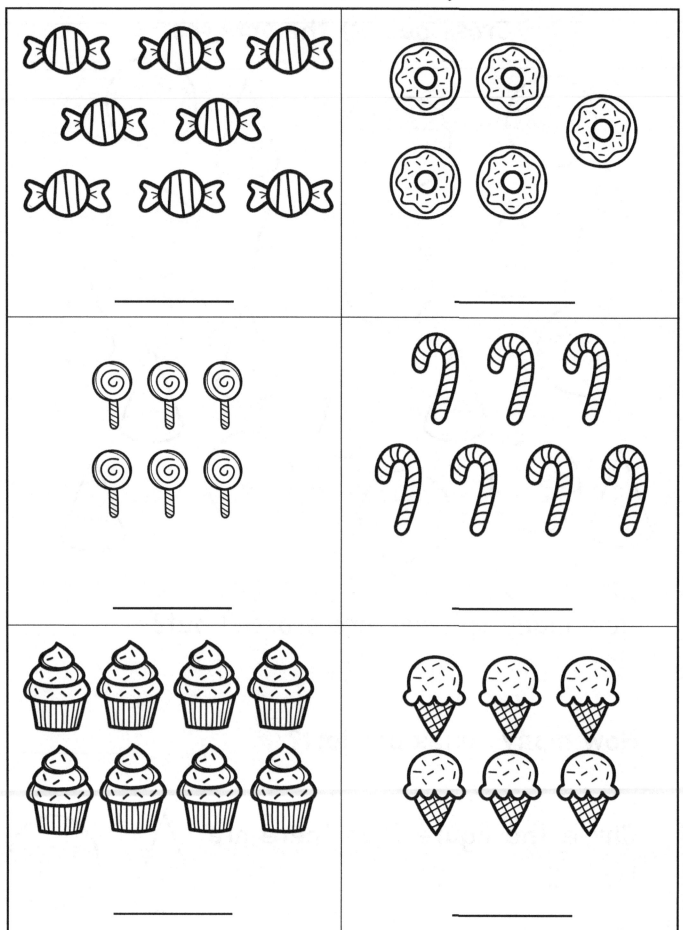

Count Backward by One
Write the missing numbers.

___ , 9 , ___ , ___ , 6 , 5 , ___ , 3 , ___ , 1

10 , ___ , 8 , 7 , ___ , ___ , 4 , ___ , 2 , ___

___ , ___ , 8 , ___ , 6 , 5 , ___ , ___ , 2 , 1

Measurement
Which is wider? Color it.

What comes next? Color it.

Figures

Cross out (x) the cylinders.

Telling Time by the Hour

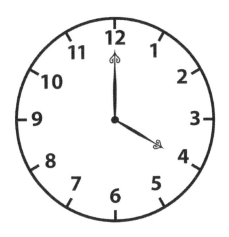

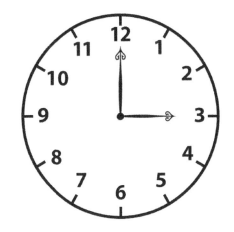

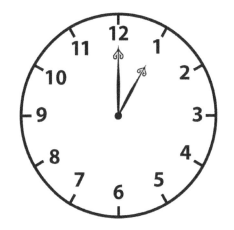

Draw a Pencil

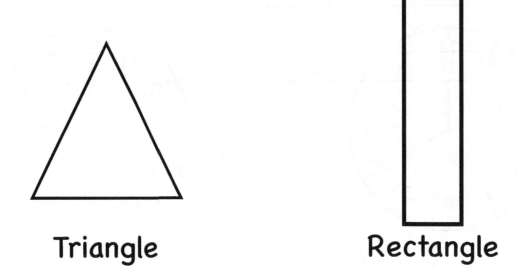

Triangle   Rectangle

Can you draw a pencil using the two shapes above?

Figures Data Collection
Color the cones.

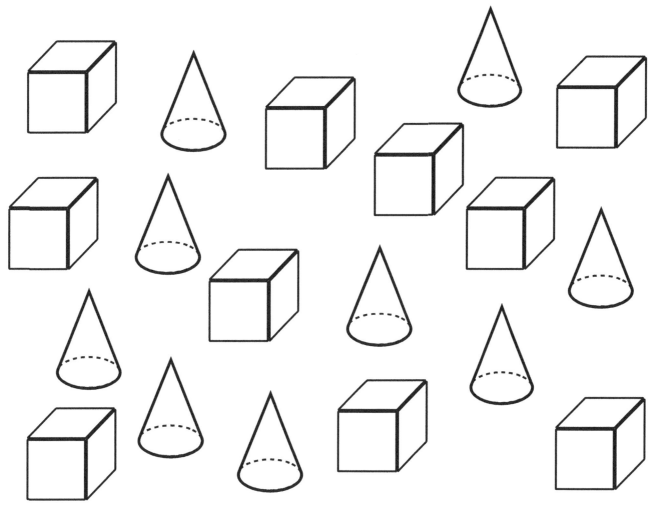

How many cones are colored?   _____

How many cubes are left?   _____

Circle the figure that there are more of.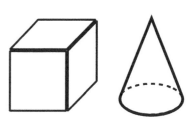

Cross out 6. How many are left?

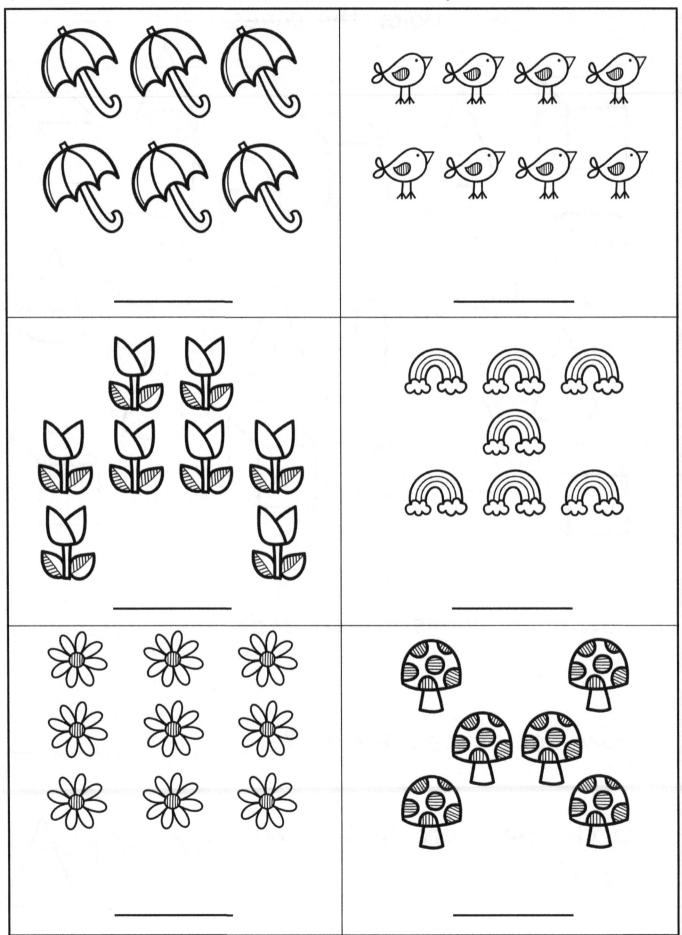

Count Backward by One

Write the missing numbers.

10 , ___ , 8 , ___ , 6 , ___ , 4 , ___ , 2 , ___

___ , ___ , 8 , ___ , 6 , 5 , ___ , ___ , 2 , 1

10 , 9 , ___ , ___ , 6 , ___ , 4 , ___ , 2 , ___

Color the water blue.
Which has more water? Circle it.

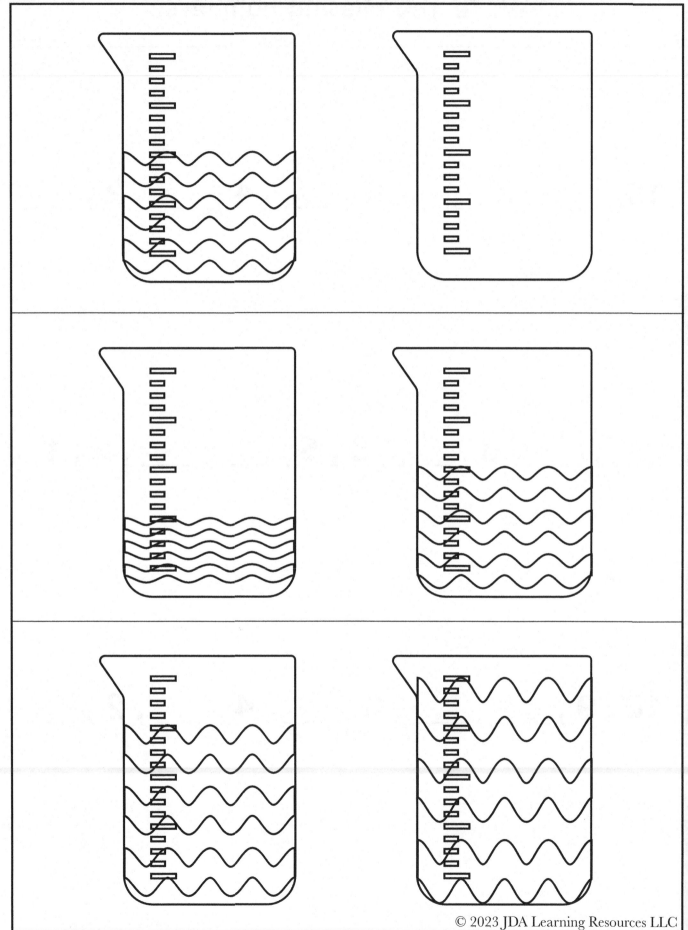

What comes next? Circle it.

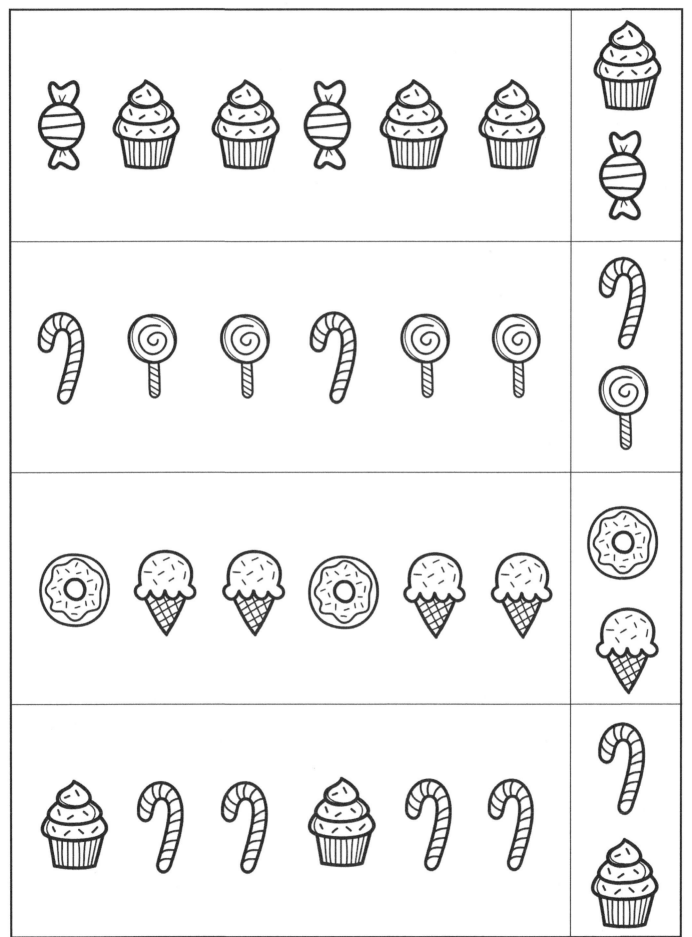

Figures
Color the spheres.

Telling Time by the Hour

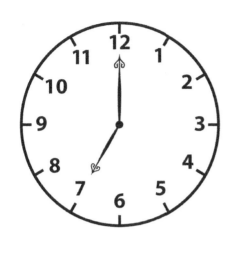

___ : ___   ___ : ___

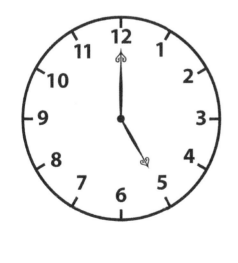

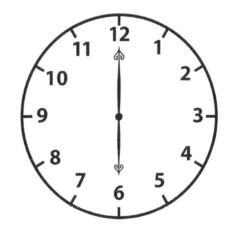

___ : ___   ___ : ___

Draw a Slice of Pizza

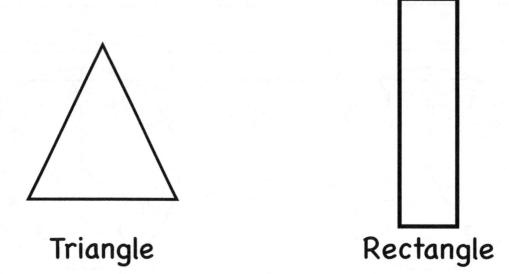

Triangle

Rectangle

Can you draw a slice of pizza using the two shapes above?

Figures Data Collection
Cross out (x) the cylinders.

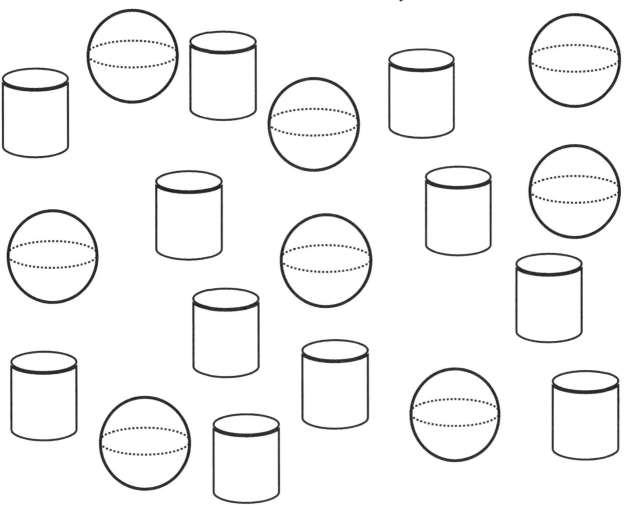

How many cylinders are crossed out?_____

How many spheres are left?　　　　　_____

Circle the figure that there are less of.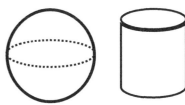

Subtraction

2 - 1 = _____

3 - 2 = _____

4 - 1 = _____

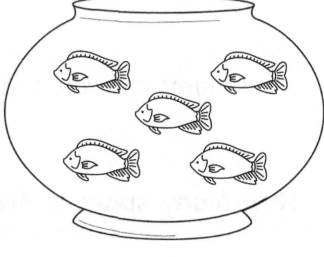

5 - 3 = _____

Color the water blue.
Which has more water? Circle it.

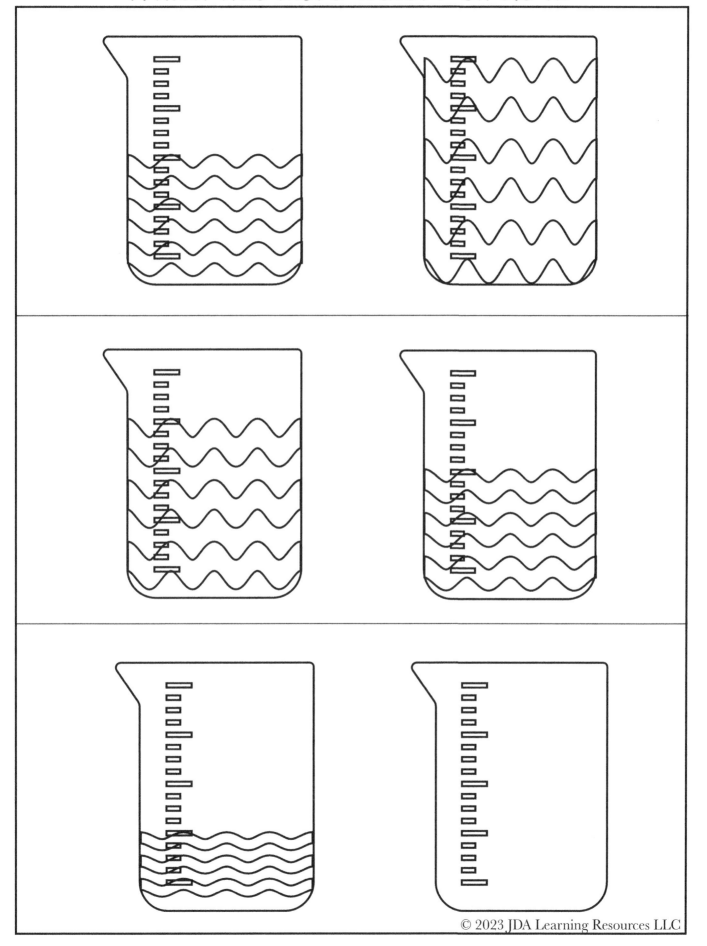

Figures

Cross out (x) the cones.

What comes next? Circle it.

Telling Time by the Hour

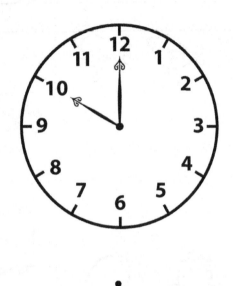

___ ___ : ___ ___   ___ ___ : ___ ___

___ ___ : ___ ___   ___ ___ : ___ ___

Symmetry
Draw a line to the other half.

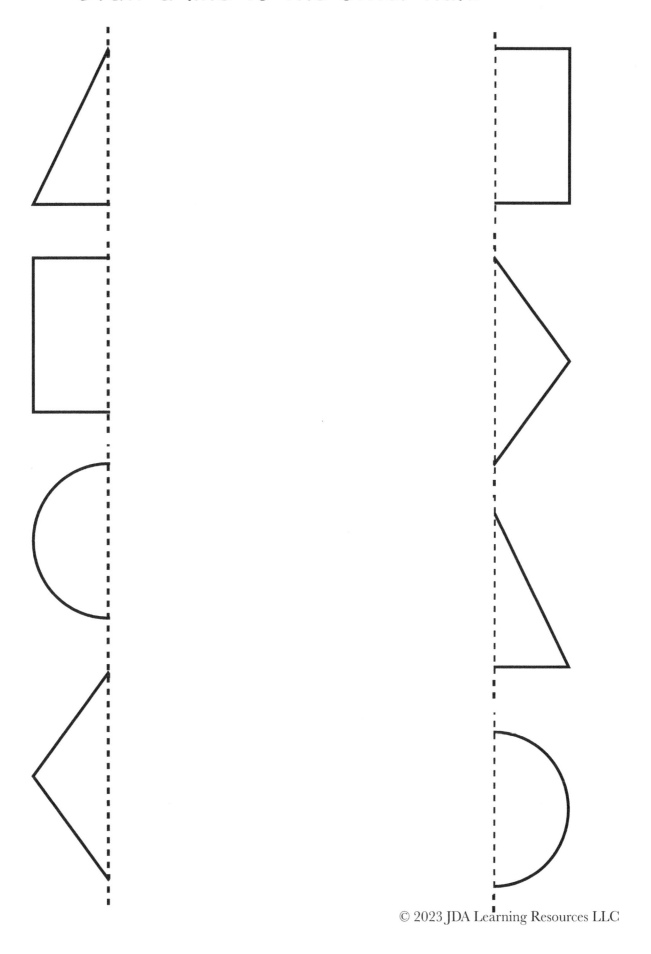

Figures Data Collection
Color the spheres.

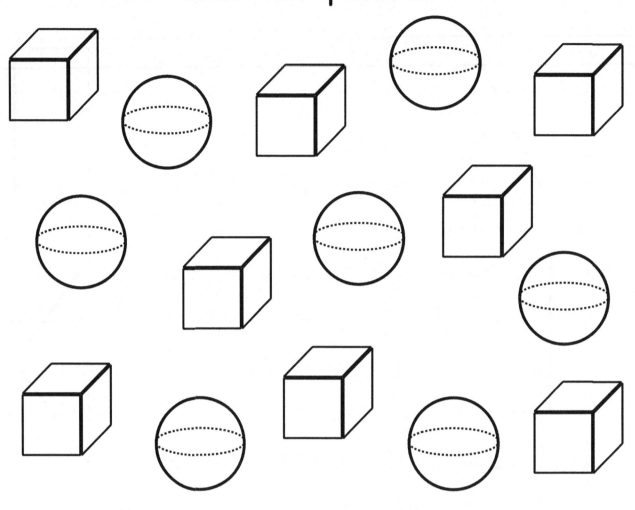

How many spheres are colored? _____

How many cubes are left? _____

Circle the figure that there are less of.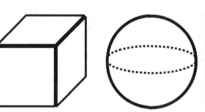

Subtraction

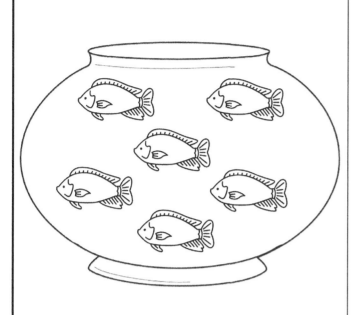

6 - 2 = _____

5 - 2 = _____

4 - 3 = _____

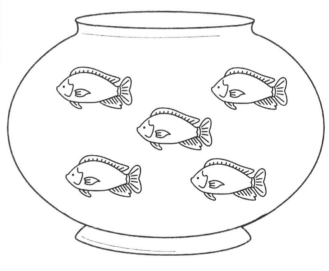

5 - 4 = _____

Color the water blue.
Which has less water? Circle it.

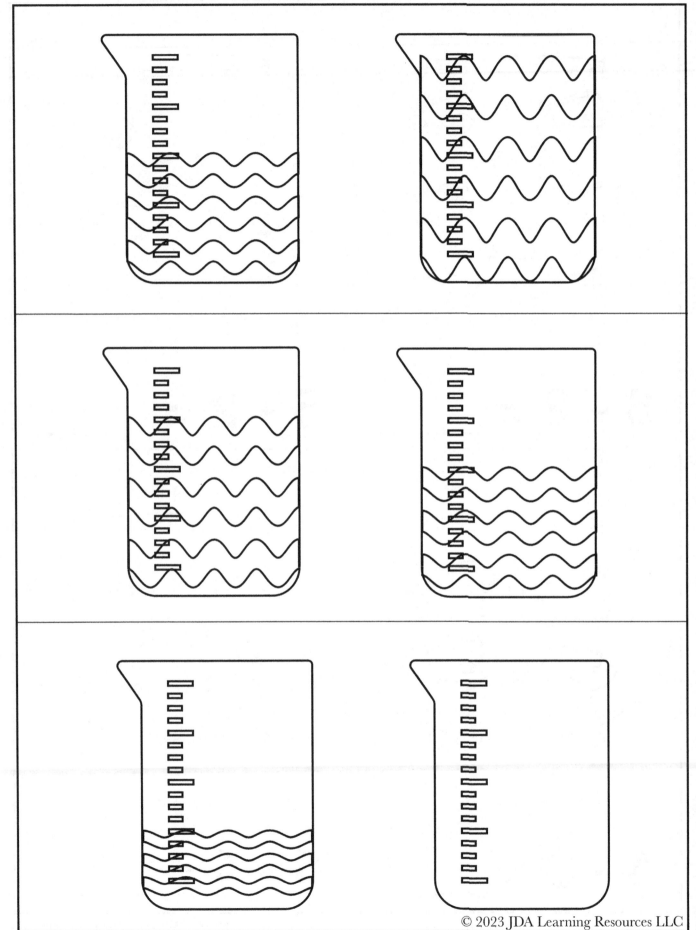

Figures
Color the cubes.

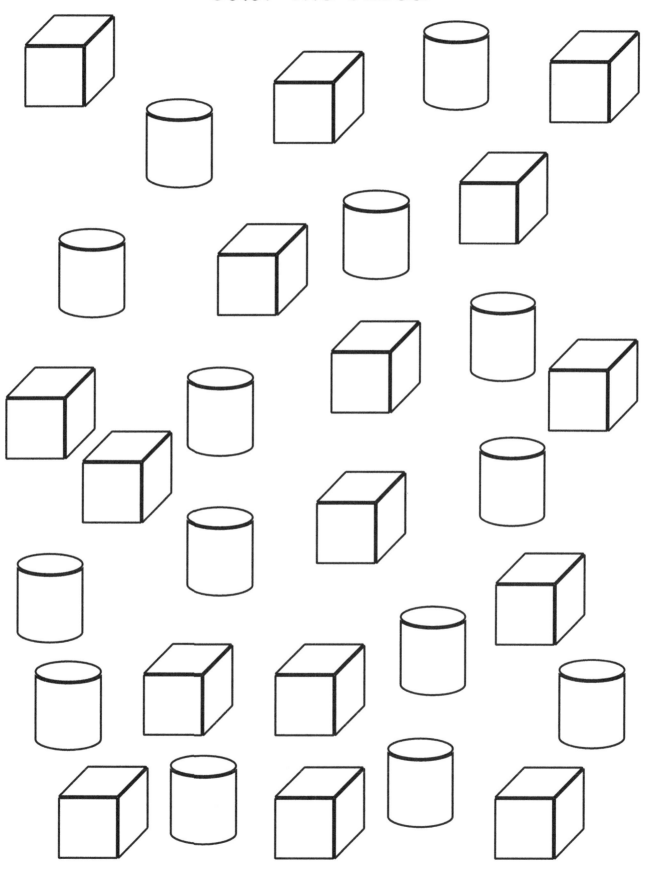

What comes next? Color it.

Telling Time by the Hour

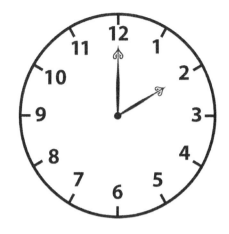

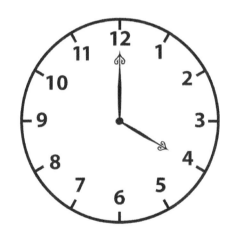

___ ___ : ___   ___ ___ : ___

Symmetry
Draw the other half.

Figures Data Collection
Cross out (x) the cubes.

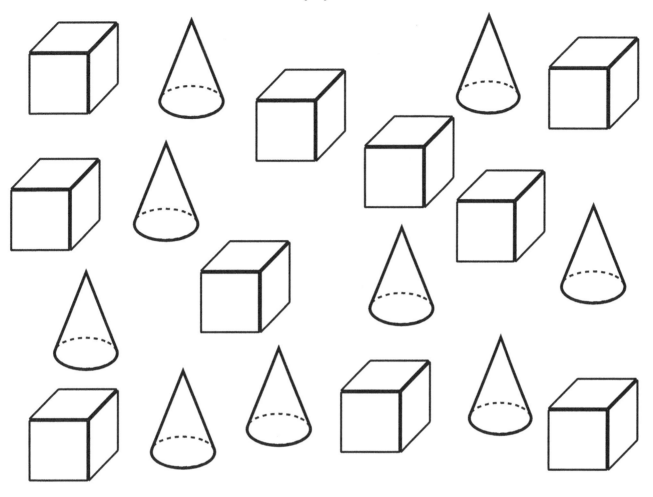

How many cubes are crossed out? _____

How many cones are left? _____

Circle the figure that there are more of.

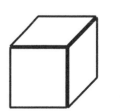 

Subtraction

_____ - _____ = _____

_____ - _____ = _____

_____ - _____ = _____

_____ - _____ = _____

Color the water blue.
Which has less water? Circle it.

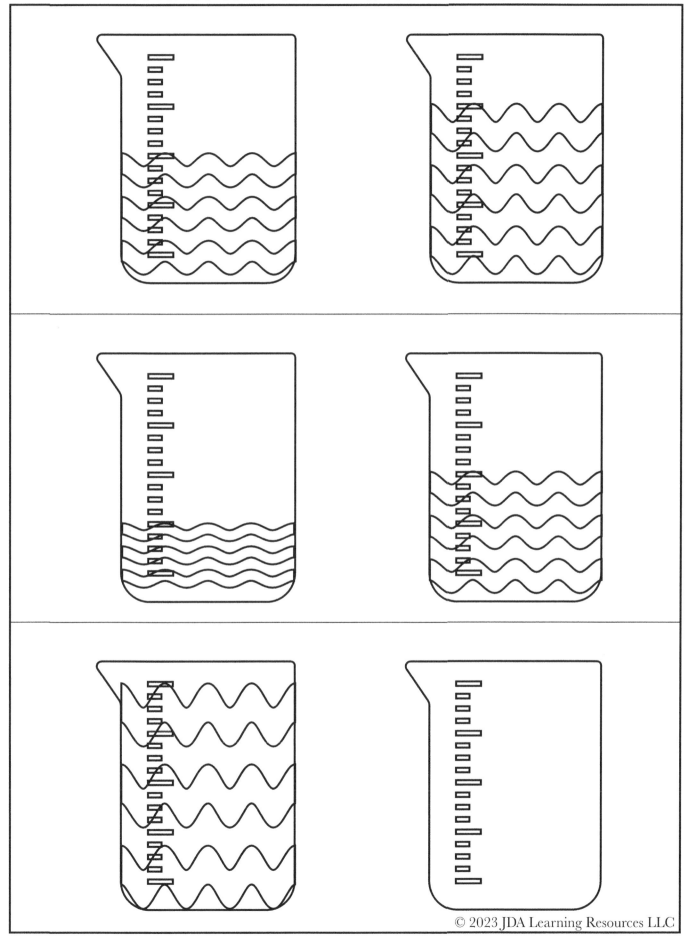

Figures
Cross out (x) the spheres.

What comes next? Circle it.

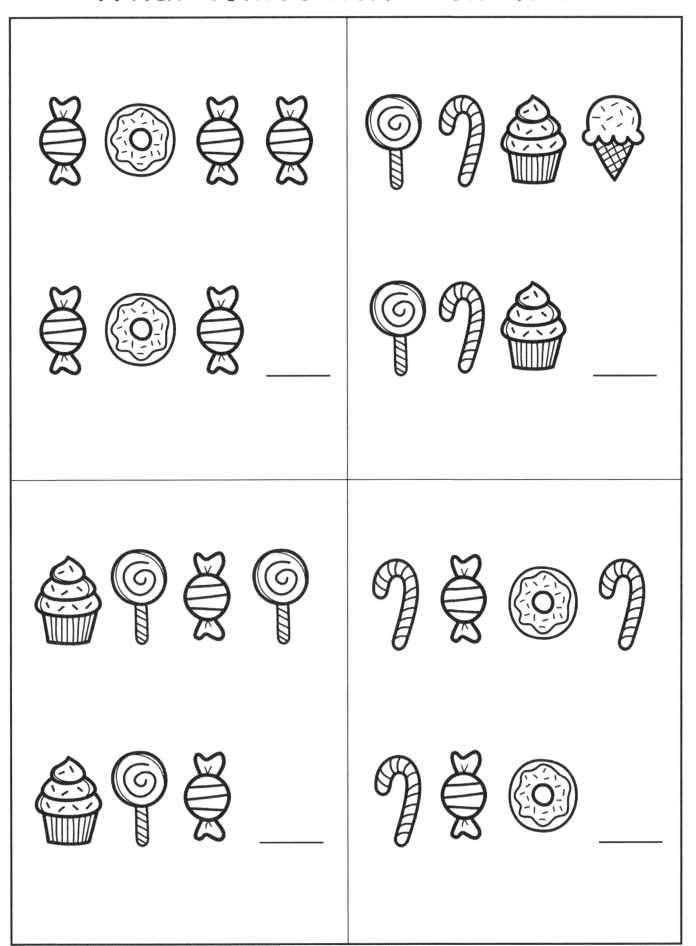

Telling Time by the Hour

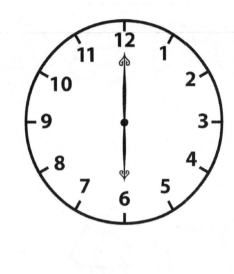

____ : ____   ____ : ____

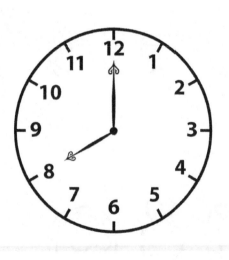

____ : ____   ____ : ____

Symmetry
Draw the other half.

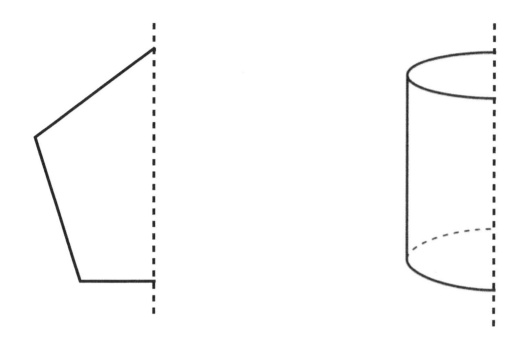

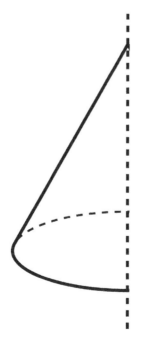

Figures Data Collection
Color the cylinders.

How many cylinders are colored? _____

How many spheres are left? _____

Circle the figure that there are less of.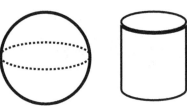

Subtraction

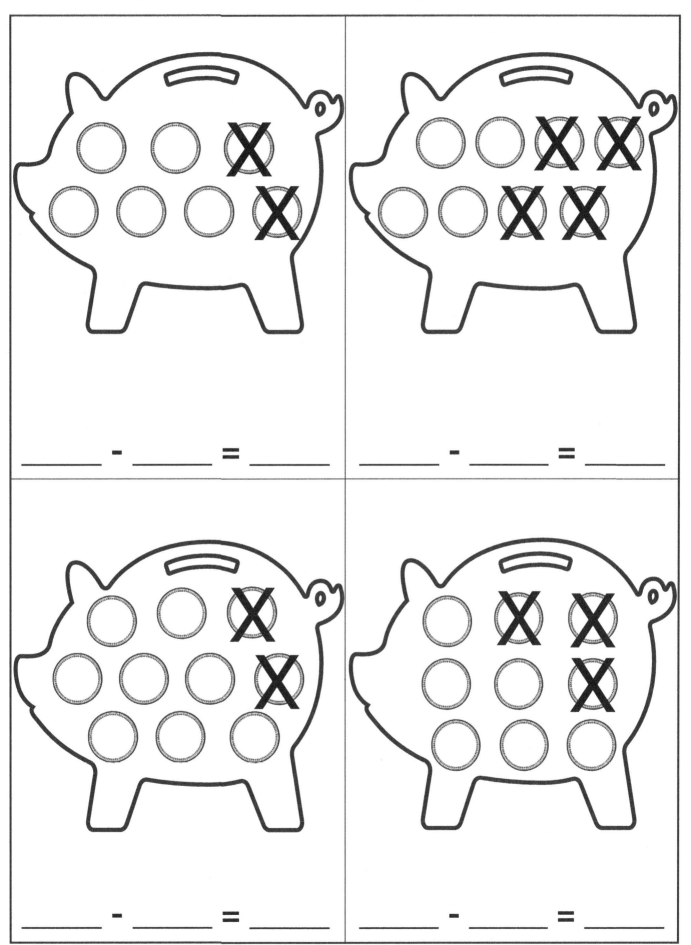

_____ - _____ = _____   _____ - _____ = _____

_____ - _____ = _____   _____ - _____ = _____

Color the water blue.
Which has less water? Circle it.

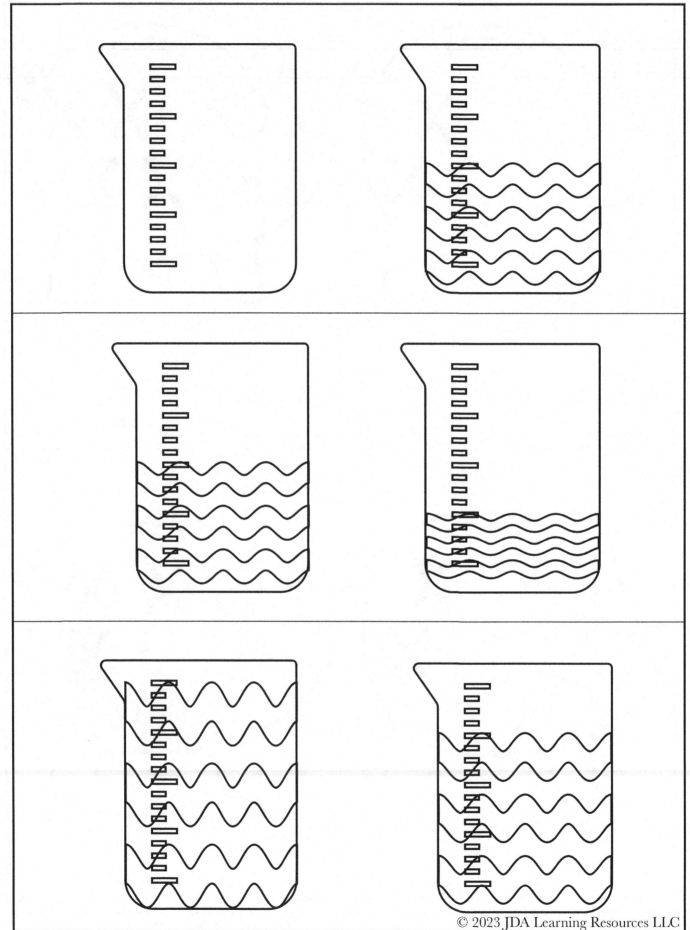

Figures
Color the cylinders.

Which is missing? Circle it.

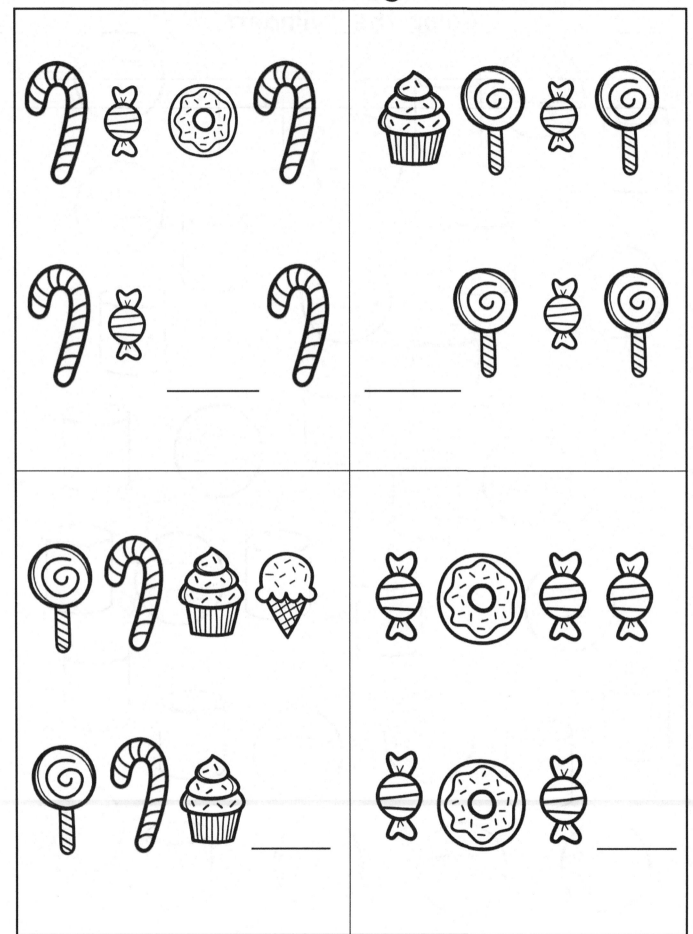

Telling Time by the Hour

_____ : _____

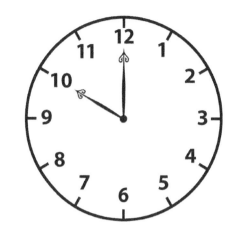

_____ : _____

_____ : _____

_____ : _____

Symmetry

Draw a picture. Make sure the drawing is the same on both sides of the dotted line.

Figures Data Collection

Cross out (x) the cones.

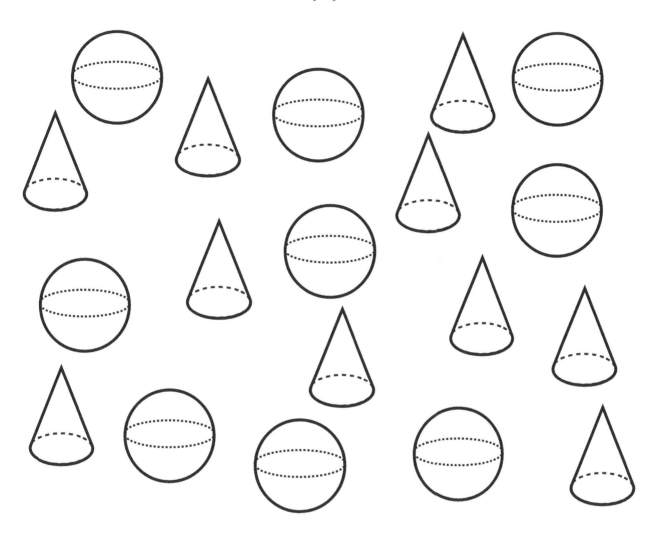

How many cones are crossed out? _____

How many spheres are left? _____

Circle the figure that there are less of.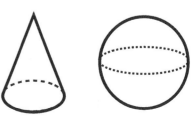

Made in the USA
Columbia, SC
22 October 2024

44800556R00089